Heaven

THROUGH THE EYES
OF CHILDREN

RICHARD FELLOWS

WORDWYZE PUBLISHING

Cover Photo:	Julia Sudnitskaya, Choreograph – istockphoto.com
Cover Design:	Bettina Kadolfer – www.bettinakadolfer.com
Co-Published by:	WordWyze Publishing – wordwyze.nz Hamilton, New Zealand

Printed Softcover edition: ISBN 978-0-648-58834-4

Dedication

To Angela Curtis, I dedicate this book to you, my friend. For without your persistence, determination, and love for God, through all the seasons, my book would not be here today. If it wasn't for your magnificent book, 'Talk With Me in Paradise', which captures the children's visions of Heaven, I would not have the major insights to write this book and go deeper. Your book is a world changer and has opened hearts around the world to God's greater love and His Kingdom. I honour you and thank you.

Contents

Preface

Books are often birthed out of experiences, and after hearing about a small community of believers in India, way up in the remote hills of an undisclosed area, that were being caught up to Heaven in full-blown spirit-body translations through visions, I decided I would take my Theologian and Apologetic mind on a mission over there to pay a visit and analyse these claims. My second night up in the jungles, staying at an Orphanage Campus, I was caught up out of my body while sitting on my bed into an open vision, where I found myself riding on a white horse to the Throne, with angels on horses riding with me. I could hear galloping all around me, and I could see both realms, earth and Heaven, simultaneously, as the Heavenly realm took me in deeper. The presence of God got stronger and stronger and overwhelming as we drew nearer the Throne. At the Throne, Jesus said to me, "And now, I will show you My Power," and the vision ended. My life has never been the same since...

It was one of the most powerful experiences into the unknown realms of my life, but it opened my heart to believe, like a child, the stories I was hearing about Heaven. In this remote area, many children in the orphanage, in worship times, were being corporately caught up to Heaven and shown the most amazing places by King Jesus. They would bring revelation back, and one by one, all share from their visions their encounters.

They would reveal the most profound places, and being very young Indian children, they knew very little of the Bible. Every night, for ten weeks, I sat listening to their stories, and as a trained Theologian, the revelation was deeper and richer than most scholars I had read. Their stories would bring Scripture texts alive to another dimension, and these children did not know this level of Theology. In fact, most adults would have to do an intense Bible study to keep up with these children, of which some were only five years old.

This season of the children being caught up daily to Heaven, for nine years, gave birth to a wonderful book called 'Talk With Me In Paradise', written by Angela Curtis.

> *"Hidden in the remote mountains of central India, a remarkable outpouring of the Holy Spirit touched a community and revealed the reality of Jesus and His Kingdom. Over 50 people were caught up into Heaven and experienced wondrous visions like the Apostle Paul."*[1]

The Children tell of the most amazing places; they have begun to map out Heaven (Eden) in their encounters. They speak of the Father, the Son, and Holy Spirit on their Throne and how they move around Heaven. They reveal Jesus' Crystal Palace, the Crystal-Ice Pipe-Organ, the Candle Room, Snow Mountain, what's under the Throne, the Father's garden, the Pool of Tears, the Wailing Flutes, the Golden Bridge to the Throne of Mercy, inside and outside the Heavenly City, and the different regions and areas of Eden, and on and on...

---

[1] Angela Curtis, Talk With Me in Paradise, Kin & Kingdoms book, 2019 – Foreword.

Some people may doubt that many of these places exist, but my Apologetic, Theologian mind has spent hours reading and researching these places the children say they have been to. Searching through Scripture, Jewish texts, Jewish traditions, Jewish sages, Biblical Scholars, and history, I have found all the places documented. These locations and places in Heaven have been deposited by revelation through a dim mirror to seekers throughout history. Some would have been there, and others would have caught the Spirit's inspiration and recorded them into writing. But the children have been there in full-blown reality, walking, seeing and touching Jesus and His Kingdom. Their insights become the higher standard of revelation, and as Jesus said, you will not see the Kingdom unless you become like a child.

In 'Heaven: Through the Eyes of Children', I document many of the places presented in the book 'Talk With Me in Paradise' and other stories I have heard from the children personally. I document them by backing them up with references producing an Apologetic, Theological mapping of Heaven.

Come, let us journey through Heaven through the eyes of children, illuminated through a Theologian's obsession and passion for seeing the Kingdom in its reality!

Our *Triune God*

The *Father*

and His *Throne*

Who is the Father? Who is the Ancient of Days? Who is the one who sits on His throne with His Son on His right side? Who is the one who walked in the Garden in Eden?

To answer these questions, we must explain somewhat the Trinity. Most of us would agree the Trinity includes the Father, Son and Holy Spirit. These three personalities (persons) are the "One eternal God" who is eternal Spirit. They have existed for all eternity before any finite creation was brought into existence.

In their Heaven encounters, the children I met in India testify that God the Father exists as a figure on a throne, mystified by a swirling rainbow mist that flows around His brightness. God the Father is not totally invisible, like some invisible consciousness. If the Father has a 'form', does that mean He is a finite (created) Being? Many scholars and philosophers would say 'Yes', but this is not the case. There is rabbinic literature that accepts the idea that God can have a body in Heaven yet still be an infinite Being.[2]

Even the early Church Father Justin Martyr criticizes the Jews in his work 'Dialogue with Trypho', for believing God could have a body (form):

"And again, when He says, 'I shall behold the heavens, the works of Thy fingers', unless I understand his method of using words, I shall not understand intelligently, but just as your teachers suppose, fancying that the Father of all, the unbegotten God, has hands and feet, and fingers, and they, for this reason,

---

[2] Alon Goshen Gottstein, The Body as Image of God in Rabbinic Literature, and Michael Fishbane, Some Forms of Divine Appearance in Ancient Jewish Thought, Bogdan B. Bucur, The Early Christian Reception of Genesis 18 from Theophany to Trinitarian Symbolism.

teach that it was the Father Himself who appeared to Abraham and Jacob."

Before we go deeper, there are some conclusions that some Evangelicals claim about God that I must reject. Yes, I reject what some Scholars and philosophers think, as I do not believe their arguments hold up. I believe they base their arguments on philosophical assumptions, without Divine, Heavenly revelation and Scriptural assertions.

*I reject the claim that an eternal spirit cannot manifest a "form/image" in creation (heaven or earth). I believe God is spirit (and will explain more later), but I don't conclude that being eternal spirit means that God is invisible in all dimensions. I believe God can take a manifested location of a form in Heaven (can be in more than one place at a time) and on earth (some might call this a theophany) and still be eternal. If God was invisible in all dimensions, how could He be a revelation revealed?

*I don't believe the Father is static on the throne and never seen anywhere else in Heaven. I don't believe the Father is stuck like a statue eternally on His throne, or 100% invisible as some define "spirit". I believe the Father can appear in different places in Heaven simultaneously.

*I believe the Father can be seen in "forms", but not His face, due to the brightness of His image. The commandment against idolatry is not due to God having no divine image. The prohibition of idolatry is about God's jealously. God does not want us to worship anything/anybody other than who He is.

*I also reject this new push to say there is no subordination of roles in the Trinity, that all have equal roles, as if the Son could crown the Father! You can have equal value, the three being one God, without saying there are no different roles or functions which each one plays that the others don't. Different roles and functions don't strip one from equal value or essence.

Defining God's Spirit: I believe God's eternal Spirit sustains all creation, but God's presence and frequency can manifest, as waves of shimming coloured light, as silhouette "forms", shadows, pillars of light, and clouds, in locations occupying space. And even human forms, Heavenly forms, theophany's, and incarnations.

Conclusions: The eternal Spirit sustaining all creation can manifest a form without the 'form' being finite. The Father can have a human-like form/shape of light on the Throne without being a finite being.

The children have reported that the Father can be on the throne, the Holy Spirit (Rainbow cloud/mist/garment of Glory) can flow around the Father on the throne, and Jesus can sit on His throne – the three are One, yet have separate forms. They also report seeing Jesus get off His throne and walk around Heaven, and the Holy Spirit (while still being around the Father), can appear as a pillar of coloured light in another part of Heaven and speak. What is also interesting is that this pillar can appear in Heaven, in different locations in Eden, and it is the Father's voice that is speaking. Sometimes the pillar of light can appear, and all three voices can be heard speaking together. The Father's tone, different than the Son's and the Holy Spirit's, are all heard– Again, the three are One.

The three are always connected as One, for there is 'One eternal Spirit' that is God, but the three have their separate personalities too (forms).

One Jewish writer says, "What is the appearance of God the Father? God is fire, and His throne is fire; clouds and fog surround Him. His face and cheeks are in the image of the Spirit, and therefore no man is able to recognise Him. But He has an image and form."

A friend's encounter seeing the Father reports:

> *"Intense light flooded out from the throne of the Father and the sound of His power made every cell in my body shake. A transparent white mist swirled around Him inside the rainbow sphere. The smell of frankincense drifted around me, touching my skin as music and worship filled the air. There was an ocean of people in white robes. Some danced before their King in worship; others lay face down on the marble floor. One by one, they removed their gem-encrusted crowns and cast them on the polished floor in an act of complete surrender. The holy presence of the Father was so thick it was hard to breathe. Waves of His power and love surged towards me. Not able to stand before Him, I bowed my knees. Light filled each person with the intensity of the Father's sovereign glory. Everything He creates is illuminated with His light, even us. It was like staring at the sun; all I could see was the dim outline of His throne and the sparks of lightning that intensified His brilliance."* [3]

---

[3] Angela Curtis, Talk With Me In Paradise, Kin & Kingdoms Publishing, 2019, p 61.

"The Ancient of Days was seated, His garment was white as snow, and the hair of His head was like pure wool. His throne was a fiery flame, its wheels a burning fire." (Daniel 7:9)

"His appearance was sparkling like crystal and glowing like a carnelian gemstone. Surrounding the throne was a circle of green light, like a rainbow." (Revelation 4:3)

Who walked in the Garden?

"And they heard a sound of the Lord God walking in the garden in the cool of the day, and Adam and his wife hid themselves from the presence of the Lord God among the trees of the garden." (Genesis 3:8)

A Heavenly Insight: It was Father God who was in the garden, moving towards Adam and Eve. When it says 'cool' of the day, the Hebrew's true meaning is "spirit/wind" (in the spirit of/in the day, a moment, He was there). The Father had turned up in a pillar of light to make fellowship. They heard the 'sound' of the (Father's) Spirit, wind, and presence approach, and they heard His voice speak out of the pillar. The Father's eternal Spirit appeared shimmering in presence, like a breeze of wind, appearing like a pillar of light hovering just off the ground that moved towards them. When it says, walking in the garden, in this instance, it was not with legs and feet, but like walking in the spirit, as we are told to do.

Take note: They all can speak through the pillar of light, the Father in the garden, The Holy Spirit in the wilderness, and the Son, in the light that shone on the road of Damascus.

Today, the Holy Spirit draws us to the Son, who then brings us to have fellowship with the Father and takes us to His throne.

Jesus said, "I am the Way, the Truth, and Life, No one can come to the Father, except through Me." (John 14:6)

Forms/Images/Likeness

* Ancient of Days, Father God, a figure, form on the throne. (Daniel 7:9)

* Holy Spirit, Rainbow Glory, Cloud, Mist, Garment around the throne. (Psalm 104:1-2; Revelation 4:2-4))

* The Son of Man – Jesus in human form, walks around Heaven and sits on His throne. (Revelation 1:1-12.14; John 3:13)

* All three sit on the throne, but they can also manifest and move to different locations.

* The Father can appear anywhere in a pillar of light and speak. Holy Spirit moves all over Heaven and earth, sometimes appearing as a pillar or cloud of glory and can speak. And at times, all three can speak through the pillar of light, their faces invisible, but their voices distinct.

* The Son, Jesus, can also appear as a bright light, like in the light on the road to Damascus. (Acts 9:3-5,17)

* Jesus can appear on earth in a disguised, morphed human form; people thought he was the gardener – *"After that, He appeared in another 'form' to two of them as they walked and went into the country."* (Mark 16:12)

* The Holy Spirit, spoken of in rabbinical thinking (as an old lady), can morph in disguised human form and move through the earth encountering people, and has never stopped doing so.[4]

---

[4] Richard Fellows, Granny Rainbow Shekinah, WordWyze Publishing, 2019.

* We will be able to see the Father one day. That is one reason Jesus came, but we will not see His face, for the light of His glory is too bright!

In the beginning, there was God. What God was doing, before all things, is an interesting question and one we can't comprehend. I believe the eternal God, the three persons of the Trinity, revealed themselves to Heaven (before the earth was created in celestial forms of glory. That is, out of their "Oneness," they manifested in "Godhead forms" to be interacted with in Heaven and later in creation. "The only begotten God, who is in the Fathers bosom, has made him known." (John 1:18). Jesus said, "I came out and came forth from God." (John 8:42). Coming out of the "Oneness" comes from the Cappadocian doctrine known as the "Perichoresis" – the doctrine of the ontological interpenetration of persons or mutual co-inherence or indwelling of persons within the Godhead – thought to be taught by Jesus in his declaration, "The Father is in Me, and I am in the Father" (John 10:38, 14:10, 17:21). Also, the Spirit of truth proceeds from the Father (John 15:26).

The eternal God can be everywhere (Omnipresent) and still appear in a "form". This is expressed in Transcendence and Immanence – two characteristics of God. God is both transcendent over and immanent in His creation, that is, God is both beyond the world and in it, but not of the world.

God the Father is the father of all creation; He is a father over all humanity, not just some. We are His sons and daughters, for we came from Him. We came from Him to be stewarded by His Son (Jesus) and transformed into their image and likeness, for they are One. We were given a birth certificate in Heaven when we came forth, and our names were written in a book of destiny. He is a Father who cares about us and has planned our lives to fulfil purpose and meaning.

"Your eyes saw my substance, being yet unformed, And in Your book, they all were written, The days fashioned for me." (Psalm 139:16)

God the Father is also a loving father over His creation; He loves all His animals. God's creatures on earth, His animals, have an awareness of their Creator; they know His voice and presence. Those in the wild know their Creator; they are far more complex than we think. In the wild, they don't know us or trust us, but they can gain this trust. Those animals which are domestic understand us far more than we think they do; they understand many languages, emotions, vibrations and intuitions of people. But it is God the Father they know without a shadow of a doubt. Humans have lost the ability to talk to animals by telepathy and interpreting sounds.

In Heaven, the animals can talk in human languages; many of the children report this. They were also able to do this before the fall. According to Josephus, all living things in the Garden of Eden spoke the same language (Antiquities 1:41). The Book of Jubilees, repeats this tradition, adding that 'on the day when Adam went out of the Garden of Eden…the mouths of all the beasts and cattle and birds and whatever walked or moved was stopped from speaking (Jubilees 3:27-28).

"Sing to the Lord with thanksgiving, Sing praises on the harp to our God, Who covers the heavens with clouds, Who prepares rain for the earth, Who makes grass grow

on the mountains. He gives to the beast its food, and to the young ravens when they cry." (Psalm 147:7-9)

"Look at the birds of the air, for they neither sow nor reap nor gather into barns; yet your heavenly Father feeds them. Are you not of more value than they?" (Matthew 6:26)

We are told that we should be kind to animals because it is a righteous action, for God loves His creation. Yes, we can eat animals with a heart of great respect, but we must not be cruel or inflict pain out of wrong motives.

"A righteous man regards the life of his animal, but the tender mercies of the wicked are cruel." (Proverbs 12:10)

There are times that God will supernaturally heal sick animals in the wild, for He loves them. There are also times that God lets animals die, for there is a season for everything under Heaven, a time to live, time to heal, and a time to die (Ecclesiastes 3:2).

"Every good gift and every perfect gift is from above and comes down from the Father of lights, with whom there is no variation or shadow of turning." (James 1:17)

The Holy Spirit

and His

Garment of Glory

In the last chapter, we read about how the children with their Heavenly encounters have seen God the Father on His throne. He has a form and can also appear as a pillar of light in different areas of Heaven. We also touched on how the Holy Spirit can appear in Heaven as a coloured rainbow pillar of light that shimmers and talks. In this chapter, we will focus on the children's account of the Holy Spirit on the throne and also His appearing and interacting with others in Heaven.

The Holy Spirit is God, a person who transcends all creation but manifests in a celestial form, radiating His presence over the throne. He also walks (hovers) as a bright Rainbow Pillar, with the likeness of the Lord, for He is the image and likeness of God (Genesis 1:26).

Speaking of the Father being clothed,

"You are clothed with glory and majesty, Who covers Yourself with light as with a garment." (Psalm 104:1-2)

The light, veil, mist, cloud around the throne is the light of the Holy Spirit clothing God the Father with glory.

"Immediately, I was in the Spirit; and behold, a throne set in heaven, and One sat on the throne. And He who sat there was like a jasper and sardius stone in appearance; and there was a rainbow around the throne, in appearance like an emerald." (Revelation 4:2-4)

Ezekiel 1:28 says, speaking of his vision of the throne,

"Like the appearance of a rainbow in a cloud on a rainy day, so was the appearance of the brightness all around

it. This was the appearance of the likeness of the glory of the Lord."

Ezekiel says that this appearance was like a bright light rainbow in a cloud, which was the Spirit of Glory. This appearance had the likeness of the Lord; it wasn't the Lord who was sitting on the throne (verse 26) but had the likeness of the Glory of the Lord. Now the Glory of the Lord is a person; it is the Spirit, the Holy Spirit, who manifests His presence. Ezekiel is saying there is one like the Lord, but also different because He was another member of the Godhead.

God said that He dwells in the thick cloud (1 Kings 8:12) – *"Clouds and darkness are round about Him; righteousness and justice are the foundation of His throne."* (Psalm 97:2) As the Father sits on the throne, the Holy Spirit clothes around Him, like a cloud veiling Him with glory. The word "darkness" means veil, which hides the full image of the Father.

While the Trinity is eternal and transcendent, their manifested "forms" can walk around Heaven, while their presence and essence still sustain all things in creation. The Holy Spirit, while around the throne, can manifest in a bodily Spirit Pillar form.

An encounter one child had in Heaven,

> *"When I opened my eyes, I was no longer in the room. I was on a riverbank in the most magnificent garden. Everywhere I looked was perfect, from the grass to the masses of bright coloured flowers. It was glorious, unlike anything I had ever seen... As I stood absorbing it all, a pillar of coloured light like a rainbow came towards me. Joy and a familiar buzz tingled through my entire body. I recognised that sensation. 'Who are you?'*

I asked, wondering if the pillar could speak, 'I am a Companion sent by God for you,' a gentle voice replied. 'You asked for me,' He said. Love surrounded me, His power so strong it was audible. Captivated, enraptured, fascinated, that's the only way I can describe it." [5]

In this encounter, we see that the Spirit of Glory around the throne appears in other areas of Heaven as a shimmering Rainbow Pillar of Light. The Holy Spirit has taken a 'form' and is speaking out of the Pillar. He is the Companion, Counsellor and Convictor in Scripture.

Because the Holy Spirit is omnipresent, He can move all around, from the throne to rainbow streaks throughout Heaven, to a bodily manifested Rainbow Pillar of light.

Some Rabbis almost went so far as bowing down to the Rainbow in the sky. They didn't see it as a finite creation, but as the Holy Spirit, Shekinah, coming from Heaven into creation.

According to Rabbi Joseph Bechor Shor (12th Century), a rainbow is not just a rainbow –refraction of light; rather, it's God's showing Himself.

The Jews say, 'Do not expect the Messiah until a Rainbow appears, radiating splendid colours throughout the world. At present, the colours of the Rainbow are dull, serving merely as a reminder that there will not be another flood. But the Rainbow that announces the Messiah will have brilliant colours and be adorned like a bride for her bridegroom. When the Rainbow appears, it will be a sign that God has remembered His covenant

---

[5] Angela Curtis, Talk With Me In Paradise, Kin & Kingdoms Publishing, 2019, p. 13.

with Israel and that the footsteps of the Messiah will soon be heard.'[6]

The Lord once instructed friends of mine to go outside their house and look in the sky. In their campus, hovering very low, was a single spectacular coloured glory cloud shimmering with rainbow colours.

> "We were so in love with the Lord, we wanted to see Him and learn more about Him. One afternoon, when Jan returned from her Heaven trip, I took her and all the kids for a walk to the pineapple garden. We enjoyed the garden then returned inside. 'The Lord wants us all to go back out to the pineapple garden again,' Jan said, not looking overly excited about the prospect. 'I'm not sure why, just that He said do it.' I didn't mind, I loved my garden. I rounded everyone up, and out we went again. 'Look up at the sky," He said. We all followed Jan's instructions, and there in the sky was a spectacular rainbow-coloured cloud hovering low over the campus. We noticed our neighbours on their rooftops trying to get a closer look at the unusual light too." [7]

These experiences have been common in Church History. The Holy Spirit was seen powerfully in Maria Woodworth-Etters's (1844-1924) ministry. One night in Dallas, Texas, while she was preaching, flames of fire in rainbow colours were seen

---

[6] https://epdf.pub/tree-of-souls-the-mythology-of-judaism.html (accessed 26/4/2021)
[7] Angela Curtis, p. 114.

around her, and a ring of light, having rainbow colours, was seen all around the tent emanating from a pillar of fire.[8]

The Holy Spirit has a form and image in Heaven and on Earth and can speak!

---

[8] Maria Woodworth-Etter, A Diary of Signs and Wonders, Chapter 70.

Jesus

and His

Crystal Palace

In the last two Chapters, we have flowed in reflection from the Father's throne to the Holy Spirit's appearances in Heaven. Now we examine Jesus' Crystal Palace. The Children in their Heavenly visits speak of being taken to a Crystal Palace of learning, where Jesus instructs and teaches Biblical truths. This Palace has many rooms dedicated to supernatural activities. Some walls surround the Palace grounds, and inside the grounds are many beautiful gardens, courtyards, and fountains. The blocks in the walls shimmer with bright coloured light reflecting out.

The children testify,

> *"I walked around the outside of the boundary wall of king Jesus' castle until I found the entrance to the palace grounds. I ran my hands along the transparent blocks with different textures of gold and raw stone. Each one shone and glowed with light inside. His golden castle stretched across miles of gardens bright with flowers and trees of all colours. Beautiful rainbows rose from the grounds stretching over the palace in all directions. Smaller rainbows started in the gardens and disappeared inside the walls... The doors were made of golden wood, and they had one bright-coloured ruby door handle each."* [9]

> *"Jesus took me to an elaborate gold fountain... It stands inside the front gate of Jesus' Palace. It is over nine feet high and each layer is intricately sculpted."* [10]

> *"In the middle was a courtyard with a big cross, made from rough wood, standing by itself, unadorned... I sighed, knowing that if Jesus was showing me, it was*

---

[9] Angela Curtis, p. 32
[10] Angela Curtis, p. 30

important. It was time for One of His lessons. On the wall of His Palace, a movie started. At least, that's what I thought it was... I was witnessing a moment in time. His time, His crucifixion." [11]

According to these accounts, Jesus has a Palace, with surrounding walls made of golden transparent crystal blocks, that the doors have ruby door handles. We are also told the Palace is a place of learning.

Is there such a place in Jewish thought?

"Seven classes will stand before the Holy Blessed One in the world to come. The first class sits in the company of the King and beholds His presence. The second dwells in the house of the King. The third ascends to the hill to meet the King. The fourth is in the court of the King. The fifth is in the Tabernacle of the King. The sixth is in the holy hill of the King, and the seventh is in the palace of the King." (Midrash on Psalms 11:7, 51a)

"Gan Eden has two gates of ruby, by which stand sixty myriads of angels. Above it are the clouds of glory, and it is smitten by four winds, so that's its odour is wafted from one end of the world to the other. Beneath it are the disciples of the sages, who expand the Torah, each of them possessing two chambers. Between every chamber hangs a curtain of glory, behind which lies Eden." (Yalkut Shimoni, Bereshit 20)

"In Gan Eden, there is a dean of the Academy in the Palace of the Nut (Hekhal Ha-Egoz). That is the Palace of Splendor, which is closed and hidden. Near it is the

---

[11] Angela Curtis, p. 30

Palace of 'the Birds Nest' and it's called the Academy. He reveals all the deep and secret things of the Torah that are made crystal clear by him."

From the beginning, the Messiah was hidden in a heavenly palace known as the Birds Nest. That is a secret place containing a thousand halls of learning.

Simcha Paull Raphael says,

"In Gan Eden, from the wall inward, there is a thick cloud, but its surroundings are brilliant. On the north side, there is a curtain that is separated from the brilliance, and a greenish fire divides them from the rest of the spirits of the garden. There the palaces are hidden because of the righteous and pure women that were in Israel. On the side of the east wind, there is a palace that is hidden and closed. It is called the Palace of Splendor. This palace is built like Heaven itself for purity, and surrounding all its walls are signs projecting and dazzling, some ascending and descending." [12]

In addition, in Upper Gan Eden, it is said that life is organized into schools or yeshivot for the learning of Torah. One image, used repeatedly to describe this region of Gan Eden, is the "Celestial Academy," yeshiva shel ma' alah (1, 7a). Within the Celestial Academy, righteous souls obtain a blissful understanding of God. Each midnight, God Himself appears within the Celestial Academy to visit and take delight in sharing His wisdom with numerous souls.[13]

---

[12] Simcha Paull Raphael, Jewish Views of the Afterlife, Rowman & Littlefield Publishers, 2019, p. 154
[13] Simcha Paull Raphael, p. 223

Howard Schwartz says,

"One of the primary traditional rewards for the righteous souls who ascended to Paradise was the opportunity to study Torah with the greatest sages of all time, including the patriarchs and great Talmudic masters. Some texts even describe the Messiah teaching Torah in His heavenly Palace."[14]

Enoch ascended on high until he reached the heaven of heavens. Then he saw a structure built of Crystal, and between those crystals were tongues of living fire. River full of living fire encircled that structure, and countless angels went in and out of that Crystal Palace (1 Enoch 71:1-14)

"When Rabbi Joshua ben Levi found himself in the Garden of Eden, he decided to explore it as completely as he could. One by one he explored the nine palaces of the Garden of Eden, until he came to the palace of the Messiah. He recognized the messiah by the splendour of his aura." (Sefer ha-Zikhronot 21;1-11; Orhot Hayim; Aggadat Bereshit 51: a-b)

Interestingly, we note that in Jesus' Library, every Biblical book that is to be birthed on earth by someone is already sitting on a shelf in Heaven. The blueprint and book is there, without a cover and title to be downloaded into the author's mind on earth in its appointed time.

"For we are His workmanship, created in Christ Jesus for good works, which God prepared beforehand that we should walk in them." (Ephesians 2:10)

---

[14] Howard Schwartz, Tree of Souls: The Mythology of Judaism, Oxford University Press, 2004, p. 190

Wendy Alec, beautifully captures the surroundings of the Crystal Palace,

"The shimmering increased tenfold, radiating from deep inside the vast range of the Golden Mountains. Outside the Palace, the outer brilliance of the radiance emanated from thousands of translucent, angelic forms and white eagles, which blanketed the vast golden mountains and translucent Crystal Palace that rose thousands of leagues beyond the white, swirling mists. When the throne and the One who sat on it had descended, the lofty, translucent pearl gates of the Crystal Palace began to open. As they did, an angelic herald blew the shofar. I heard the holy Council of the Ancient Ones. He proclaimed, 'Stewards of Yehovah's mysteries'." [15]

---

[15] Wendy Alec, The Fall of Lucifer, Warboys Publishers, 2008, p.15

Dancing
in the
Refining
River of Fire

There is a refining fire in Heaven that moves around to different locations where people can dance in its flames and find healing from trauma. This fire is the presence of God, a tangible manifestation, and flows from the throne, swirling around the throne to into the river, but also it appears in a room in Jesus' Palace and in His garden. The fire does no physical harm to those who bath in it and dance.

The children testify,

"When I reached Heaven, I was standing in the fire before the throne of God," Andie said. "There were angels and people dancing all around me and worshipping the Lord." [16]

"Music comes out of the fire. If the music is fast, we dance really fast. If it's slow, we dance slow. Sometimes, I dance with the angels or Jess. The other girls from the hostel are there, too. We lost our home in my village, and I felt very sad about it. When I went to the fire to dance, Jesus removed all my sadness. When I dance now, I feel happy, and I laugh…" Anna said.

Esther said, "I go there to dance. It's about thirty feet around. I usually dance with angels and Jesus…"

Jase explained, "The fire is a place of purification. The children who go there are most often the ones who have suffered physical or emotional trauma. This is where Jesus cleanses them and replaces their pain with healing and joy." [17]

---

[16] Angela Curtis, p. 84
[17] Angela Curtis, p.58

*"And there were seven lamps of **fire** burning before the **throne**, which are the seven spirits of God." (Revelation 4:5)*

"A Fiery stream came before Him" another translation says "A river of fire streamed forth before Him, a thousand thousand ministered before Him" (Daniel 7:10)

From the throne, fire streams from it, like a river. It is a fire that does not consume but floods the presence of God around the throne and then fades down into the River of Life. Children, Adults, and those who have experienced traumas often get caught up to Heaven to the throne to dance and sing in this fire. They are illuminated with the light of God and bathe in the fire, dancing and praising in the flames.

Howard Schwartz says,

"Before they can sing before God, all the angels must go and bathe in the fire, then they encircle the Throne of Glory, singing hymns of praise to God. The River of Fire can restore as well as destroy. The river serves as the heavenly "mikveh", the ritual bath in which all souls are immersed. In this way, all impurities are burned up. The souls of the righteous are ritually immersed in this stream, removing all impurities." [18]

"For he is like a refiner's fire...He will sit as a refiner and a purifier of silver; He will purify the sons of Levi, and purge them as gold and silver. That they may offer to the Lord an offering in righteousness." (Malachi 3:2-4)

---

[18] Howard Schwartz, p. 158

35

As the children danced in the fire, their behaviour and sadness changed to joy:

> *"After Rebeka had been through the refining by fire, she told everyone she met about Jesus and of His love for them. The change in her was remarkable. We noticed when the children danced during their open visions, their dancing was so vigorous, sweat poured off their natural bodies. We also learned that the fire moved to different areas of Heaven, not just in the Palace."*[19]

> *"If Jesus or the angels tell us to go to the fire in the garden, we go there and dance,"* Anna said. *"Even though we are inside the fire, we don't get hot, just a little bit warm."*[20]

Simcha Paull Raphael says,

> *"Upon entering Upper Gan Eden, the soul is once again immersed in the celestial River of Light, nehar dinur. This second immersion heals the soul and purges it of any remaining defilements."* [21]

> *"You have turned my mourning into dancing."* *(Psalm 30:11)*

Illuminated by LIGHT!

> *"Intense light flooded out from the Throne of the Father, and the sound of His power made every cell in my body shake. The smell of frankincense drifted around me, touching my skin as music and worship filled the*

---

[19] Angela Curtis, p.57
[20] Angela Curtis, p.57
[21] Simcha Paull Raphael, Jewish Views of the Afterlife, Rowman & Littlefield Publishers, 2019, p.222

air... Light filled each person with the intensity of the Fathers sovereign glory. Everything He creates is illuminated with His light, even us." [22]

Our spirit bodies become fully illuminated by God's light, and we become garments of light. As Jesus said, 'You are the Light of the World.' (Matthew 5:14)

In Proverbs 20:27 it says of our spirit body,

> *"The spirit of a man is the lamp of the LORD, searching out his inmost being."*

Adam became a living being on earth, and the light of his spirit shone through his temple body and overshadowed it like a glowing, glorious robe of light.

> *"For He has clothed me with garments of salvation (robes of glory), As a bridegroom decks himself with ornaments, and a bride adorn herself with her jewels." (Isaiah 61:10)*

> *"For you were once in darkness, but now you are light in the Lord. Live as children of light." (Ephesians 5:8)*

Howard Schwartz says,

> *"When Adam and Eve were first created, they were clothed, body and soul, with garments of light. Some say those garments of light were made entirely of clouds of glory, others like a radiance torch, broad at the bottom and narrow at the top."*

Sources: Targum Pseudo-Yonathan on Genesis 27;15; B. Pesahim 54a; Genesis Rabbah 20;12; Numbers Rabbah 4;8;

---

[22] Angela Curtis, p.61

Pesikta de-Rabbi Eliezer 20;46a, 22;50b; Pesikta de-Rav Kahana; Pesikta Rabbati 37; Midrash Tanhuma, Toledot 12; Aggadat Bereshit, Sefer ha- Zikhronot 1;3; Zohar 1;53a, 1;73b-74a, 2;229b; Ben Yehoyada; Shi nei Luhot ha-B'rit, va-yeshev; Kedushat Shabbat 5;13b."[23]

The Church Father Arnobius of Sicca, AD326, in his work Against Heathens" - wrote,

> *"But let us not reason from things terrestrial as regards things celestial, our coarse material fabrics are "shadows of the true." The robes of light are realities, and are conformed to spiritual bodies, as even here a mist may envelop a tree."*

The Church Father Methodius, AD280, in his comments on Isaiah 60 wrote,

> *"Arise and shine, for thy light is come, and the glory of the Lord is risen upon thee. It is the Church whose children shall come to her with all speed after the resurrection, running to her from all quarters. She rejoices, receiving the light which never goes down and clothed with the brightness of the Word as with a robe. For with what other more precious or honourable ornament was it becoming that the Queen should be adorned, to be led as a Bride to the Lord, when she had received a garment of light, and therefore was called by the Father."* [24]

---

[23] Howard Schwartz, p.438

[24]

https://biblehub.com/library/methodius/the_banquet_of_the_ten_virgins_or_concerning_chastity/chapter_v_the_woman_who_brings.htm

Mike Parson tells us there are many rooms and thrones in Heaven,

> *"I discovered that there are many rooms in the mountain of God and different places. There are many thrones and different places of government. There are many thrones of God where God dwells and many thrones where we can be seated. There is the throne of the Ancient of Days, by the fire stones. There is the throne in the temple, where the train of His robe fills the temple. There is the mercy seat, where the presence of God manifests the four faces of God. Then there is the throne room, where we get the lightning and thunders, the four living creatures and the 24 elders. It is different places because there are different functions in heaven."* [25]

---

[25] Mike Parson, My Journey Beyond Beyond, The Choir Press, 2018, p. 105

The Father's Garden and the Pool of Tears

On our journey so far, we have explored the Father's "form" in Heaven and His throne, the Holy Spirit's appearances in Heaven, Jesus' Palace, and the refining fireplaces, starting at the Throne and throughout Heaven, where healing takes place. In this chapter, we will explore what is under God's throne. I have a friend who has been there many times, but revelation of this place is still quite a mystery.

From the foundation stone in Heaven upon the Mountain is God's throne, of which the eternal living water of life flows. Many scriptures talk of God's throne, from different sides leading to different places, but what is under God's throne?

"Adam discovered a garden paradise in Eden by a great sea. He was blessed with wisdom and knowledge to build a palace with lavish gardens on top of the mountain. A serrated, emerald peak punctured the sky as rivers of living water flowed from the Throne above. They poured out through a celestial spout cutting creases into the mountain's limestone rock. The water funnelled down through rocky outcropping to empty into a deep sea, crystal pool. A Sapphire mist embraced the rocks; its tentacles hovered along primordial pathways. Massive obsidian pillars supported quadrangular arches to provide shade for the walkways underneath. Stairways carpeted in brilliant light reached up to multi-tiered platforms that showcased a profusion of trees, shrubs, and vines. In the centre of the garden were two pillars, two trees, the Tree of Life and the Tree of the Knowledge of Good and Evil. The trees sprouted up from the ground near the Gihon springs; their deep

roots drank from the eternal foundation. The great canopy from the Trees provided great shade." [26]

Adam and Eve would go up the Mountain to worship the Lord at His throne, and then they would descend a little along well-travelled paths to the Gihon spring in the valley below – a sacred spot that featured the spring known as the "fountain of living water". Crystal clear waters would bubble up from deep inside the subterranean cavern.

"And He showed me a pure river of water of life, clear as crystal, proceeding from the Throne of God and of the Lamb." (Revelation 22:1)

"Who may go up on the mountain of the Lord? Who may stand in His Holy Place? One with clean hands and a pure heart." (Psalm 24:4)

The River of Life flows from the throne, down through the Father's Garden and down the Mountain. Not only are there pathways down the Mountain, but the living waters have cut channels into the Mountain, like pillars where a cave growing a forest and bush exists under the throne in the Rock. It is God's inner chamber inside the Rock.

"For in the time of trouble, He shall hide me in his inner chamber. In the secret place of His sanctuary, He shall hide me, and He shall set me high upon a rock." (Psalm 27:5)

---

[26] Dinah Dye, The Temple Revealed in the Garden, Foundations in Torah Publishers, 2017, p.28

Caves in the ancient world represented the inner sanctum of a temple. A Cave or tomb inside a mountain was a symbol for the temple's sacred centre.[27]

Under the throne, through the forest, there is a big pool of water called the "Pool of Tears". This is where all our tears shed on earth are collected and formed. Some are collected in glass bottles, and others form in the pool into precious stones.

> *"You keep track of my wanderings and my weeping. You have stored my many tears in your bottle – not one will be lost. For they are recorded in your book of remembrance." (Psalm 56:8)*

My friend explains more from their experiences from under the throne,

> *"I have seen the place where our tears have been collected in reflective glass jars of all sizes. The Lord takes me there when He wants me to sit and listen to what's on His heart. I've been there numerous times when I was concerned about someone at the campus. Sometimes, He shows me a bottle and tells me why they were shed. We pray together over the situation, and He sends His angels to answer the person's prayers. There is a huge body of water like a lake that is called the tears pool. It is where our tears are collected when we cry out to God in intercession for others. The angels told me that Jesus' tears are also in this pool. They are added when He walks through the valleys by our side and cries with us. Jesus taught me, the tears in the bottles are incredibly powerful; and how they are used by angels*

---

[27] Dinah Dye, p. 101

for spiritual warfare and how some turn into precious stones after our prayers have been answered. Those sparkling gems are placed into a special wall so exquisite; I couldn't help but be moved. Especially knowing these tears have come from someone weeping in pain." [28]

Rabbi Kalonmus Shapira says that God weeps in His innermost chamber,

"For if you will not heed, My inmost self must weep in secret because of your arrogance." (Jeremiah 13:17)

B.Berrakhot 59a says; that God's tears flow down His fingers into an ocean pool that builds spiritual power to be released on the earth.

A 2nd Century Rabbi reveals this place as well - Yitzchak Vorker,

"Before Reb Yitzchak Vorker left this world, he promised his son that he would contact him from heaven and tell him how things were for him in Gan Eden. But four weeks passed, and his son didn't hear from him. He couldn't understand what was going on, so he went to his father's best friend, Reb Menachem Mendel of Kotsk, and said: 'Rebbe, I'm so worried about my holy father. He promised to come back and speak to me, if only in a dream. But it's been four weeks, and I haven't heard anything from him. Do you think something could have happened to him in Heaven?'

---

[28] Angels Curtis, p.83

"And the Kotzker answered. 'The truth is that your father also promised me to come back and tell me what happened to him in the World Above. And I got worried when I didn't hear from him. So, I went up to Heaven to look for him.

"Let me tell you what happened: I went everywhere in Heaven searching for your father. I went to the palaces of all the tzaddikim, all the holy people – of Rashi, the Rambam, Rabbi Akiva. I visited the place of the prophets, and even went to the very highest levels – to Moshe Rabbeinu and our holy fathers, Abraham, Isaac and Jacob. Everywhere I went, I said, 'I'm looking for my friend, the exalted Reb Yitzchak Vorker. Have you seen him?' And they all told me, 'Yes, he was here. But he didn't stay. He went on...'

"I didn't know what to do, where else to go. So finally, I asked the angels, 'Have you seen the holy Reb Yitzchak Vorker? Do you know where he went?' And this time I got an answer, the angels told me, 'If you keep going in this direction, you'll come to a thick dark forest. You must pass through it, and when the forest ends at a sea, that's where you'll find him.'

"So, I kept walking through Heaven, and as the angels had said, I soon came to the darkest, most forbidding forest I had ever seen in my life. I wanted to run away. I started to hear a strange sound.

"Finally, I came out of the trees and found myself on the shore of the sea, an ocean so big I couldn't see the other side. And I realized that the sound I'd been hearing was coming from the waves. But it was not the sound that waves usually make... it was more like a wail, a moan,

*a scream – full of the most desperate pain. Never in my
life had I heard waves crying and begging like this...
And there at the edge of the ocean, I saw your father,
the holy Vorker. He was leaning on his staff, staring at
the sea. He never took his eyes off the water. I ran
toward him, 'Reb Yitzchak, my holy friend, what is this
place? What are you doing here?' He turned towards
me, 'Ah Mendel, don't you recognize this ocean?'*

*"'No, what is it? What's that sound? What's going on
here?'*

*"'Mendel, let me tell you...this is the Ocean of Tears,
the sea of Jewish tears. I want you to know that
every tear is so precious to the Master of the World.
God takes all the tears and places them here. And
there were so many tears – that they formed this
huge ocean... When I came here and heard the
sound of the waves, the cry of all the suffering of so
many, I can't tell you how much it broke my heart. And
at that moment, I made a sacred vow: "Master of the
World, I swear to you by Your Holy Name that I will not
move from this place until You have mercy on your
people until you turn all the pain to joy." 'My dear
friend,' said the holy Rebbe, 'I will never leave
this Ocean until God has wiped away all of the tears.'"*
[29]

As the water flows down from the throne, we are told it flows
down the Mountain, into valleys, springs and pools; that there is
a tunnel that goes under the throne to the Father's Garden. My
friend has told me it's like a forest going under, but you come out

---

[29] Shmuel, The Ocean of Tears, Tikkun, accessed 22 Apr 2021,
http://loveisthemotive.blogspot.com/2014/10/the-ocean-of-tears.html

to a big lake of water, the Pool of Tears. The 2nd century Rabbi also describes a forest in his account quoted above. This Ocean of Tears is the sea of all our tears. Every tear is so precious to the Father. God collects all the tears and stores them here. And there are so many tears that they have formed this huge ocean.

The Talmud says, "Whosoever sheds tears at the death of a good man, the Holy One counts them and stores them away in His Treasure House. You have counted my wanderings, put my tears in your flasks, and are they not already in your ledger?"

God treasures the tears of the broken-hearted.

It's interesting to note that Mike Parson, from his Heavenly encounters, said in the previous chapter, that *"He discovered that there are many rooms in the mountain of God and different places".*

Under the throne, on the Mountain of God, inside the "Rock", there are many rooms and different places. This would include the treasure house and the cave that leads through the forest to the garden where the pool of tears is. My friend also says, *'those sparkling gems are placed into a special wall'.* Again, this would be in the treasury room or store house.

In 'Ein Ya Akeov Hotza At Sefa', it says, "He places them (tears) in His House of Treasure in order to use them for the resurrection of life."

"Jesus taught me, the tears in the bottles are incredibly powerful; and how they are used by angels for spiritual

warfare and how some turn into precious stones after our prayers have been answered." [30]

"You intended to harm me, but God intended it for good to accomplish what is now being done, the saving of many lives." (Genesis 50:20)

A Jewish Proverbs says, "A Drop of Love can bring an ocean of tears." (Yiddish).

"Jesus wept. Then the Jews said, see how He loved him!" (John 11:35)

---

[30] Angela Curtis, p. 83

Tears
Forming
Gems
and Wailing
Flutes

In the last chapter, on the "Pool of Tears", I revealed that under the throne, deep under is a pool of water from the crystal sea that collects our earthly tears. In this pool, precious stones are "formed" as stones of remembrance, and they are collected by angels and put into a treasury room. Many of our tears are also collected and sealed into little bottles. These tears are a remembrance of the pain and love that has been spilt for the Lord's heartbeat. These tears in the pool hold a frequency and are poured out many times in warfare on our behalf, and the precious stones once fully formed are then placed on a huge wall of remembrance of victories gained in answered prayer.

> *"Jesus taught me, the tears in the bottles are incredibly powerful; and how they are used by angels for spiritual warfare and how some turn into precious stones after our prayers have been answered. Those sparkling gems are placed into a special wall so exquisite; I couldn't help but be moved. Especially knowing these tears have come from someone weeping in pain".* [31]

With the precious stones mounted in it, the wall in Heaven is the Heavenly copy of the "Wailing Wall" of the Temple on earth. Jewish tradition says that every morning, drops of dew can be seen on its stones, and it was said that at night the Wall was crying. They say women collected the tears of the Wall as precious remedies for many ailments, spiritual remedies. [32]

Wendy Alec, in her book Visions of Heaven, also reveals the glass canisters of tears in her Heavenly encounter,

---

[31] Angela Curtis, p.83
[32] Richard Fellows, Wilderness Like Eden, WordWyze Publishing, 2019, p. 144

"The Father picked up the most exquisitely cut-glass canister filled to the brim with liquid. 'These are your tears that you shed during your time of intense trial.' He picked up another much, much larger canister. 'And, these are the tears that I shed, For you.' And the Father lifted the canister of His tears and poured them over the blood seeping from my heart. Instantly the blood stopped flowing, and a great comfort washed over my heart." [33]

Another revelation I was given was that flutes form and float in the pool to be collected. On hearing this revelation, I didn't know what to do with it, so I had to sit on it for a time for understanding.

The flutes in the water also form from our tears of great weeping and wailing and are used by the Lord. Jesus said, that if no one praised him, even the rocks would cry out. This is true. As the stones in the pool in Heaven are made from our tears, they cry out in frequency, and if Jesus wanted to, the very stones on earth would cry out as well.

In Jeremiah 48:36, it hints that flutes cry out and wail and weep deep from the heart. These Heavenly flutes created and formed by our tears, wail a deep sound and frequency in mourning, until the Lord uses them to sound joy and victory.

"Therefore, my heart shall wail like flutes for Moab, and like flutes, My heart shall wail." (Jeremiah 48:36)

---

[33] Wendy Alec, Visions of Heaven, Warboys Publishing, 2013, p. 25

"Then they came to the house of the ruler of the synagogue and saw a flute and those who wept and wailed loudly." (Mark 5:38)

"We played the flute for you, and you didn't dance, We mourned for you, and you didn't lament." (Matthew 11:17)

The flute in Scripture is used for times of mourning and also for times of joy and refreshing. In Heaven, these flutes are used by the Lord as He puts His breath (life) into our tears and brings forth a sound of victory.

According to a Jewish Midrash, when God sees a suffering child, He drops two tears into an ocean. When it hits the ocean, the sound is so powerful that you can hear it all around.

*"And, behold, the glory of the God of Israel came from the way of the east: and his voice was like a **noise of many waters:** and the earth shone with his glory." (Ezekiel 43:2) (emphasis mine)*

*"Then I heard what seemed to be **the voice** of a great multitude, like the roar of **many waters** and like **the sound** of mighty **peals of thunder**, crying out, "Hallelujah!" (Revelation 19:6) (emphasis mine)*

The stones, rocks, tears, waters, and flutes cry out, formed by the waters of the pool. As God drops His tears into the pool, the sound of thunder and many ripples flood through the waters, and ministers to those to whom the tears belong. The water speaks, and also those who are in Heaven cry out in praise to God. The manifest Sons of Glory cry out!!! The Sons of Thunder cry out! The peals of Thunder cry out!

Sounds and instruments move God in Heaven. There is a belief found in 'Pesikta de-Rav Kahana' that the sounding of the shofar causes God to move from His throne of Justice to the throne of Mercy.[34]

---

[34] Howard Schwartz, p. 297

The Crystal

Pipe

Organ

on

Snow Mountain

In Eden, not far from the throne and Jesus' Palace, there are mountain ridges that surround the Hill of the Lord. One mountain is said to be covered with shimmering gold dust, and another to be covered with snow. Snow exists just under the throne, and on this one mountain, called, 'Snow Mountain'. The children testify from their Heaven encounters that there is a "Crystal Ice Pipe-Organ" that plays beautiful music on its own on this mountain.

One child's testimony:

> *"I have amazing new friends, a horse. She is white and has huge feathered wings. My horse comes to the prayer hall, and I ride up to Heaven. She likes to take to me to the Throne Room, the Music Realm and the Snow-covered Mountain, where there is a pipe organ made of ice. It plays beautiful music all by itself."* [35]

Let me set some context. This child is in the prayer room on earth and is suddenly caught up to Heaven in a vision. The child's 'spirit body' literally is caught up in the spirit realm and finds itself appearing on a white horse riding up to the throne. She rides upon a Heavenly white horse to the throne room. The throne room is in the Temple, and near the Temple is the sanctuary, and just under the throne on a huge mountain ridge is snow (Snow Mountain), where we are told a pipe organ made of ice exists and plays by itself. While I was in India, I had a very similar experience of riding on a Heavenly horse.

Does this account of the organ correspond to Jewish thought?

---

[35] Angela Curtis, p. 41

One of the instruments used in the Temple, according to Jewish authorities, is the magreifah, a kind of organ, and is described to be a square box, with an extension on the side (possibly for keys or for bellows), from which 10 pipes extend with 10 holes in each. Considering that each hole could be open or closed in combination with the others, this allowed for thousands of chords to be played through this organ. Our pipe organs of today may be based on this idea.[36]

As I always say, as below, so above, as above, so below. The earth is a copy of above – Heaven.

"But Jerusalem above is free, and she is our mother."
(Galatians 4:26)

Now let's look at the account of the mountains in these visions:

" 'This is Snow Mountain,' He said smiling. Some of the mountains are covered with gold dust, others with sparkling ice crystal." [37]

Wendy Alec captures the scenery of these mountains in her visons,

"The Shimmering increased tenfold, radiating from deep inside the vast range of the Golden Mountains. Outside the palace, the outer brilliance of the radiance emanated from thousands of thousands of translucent, angelic forms and white eagles, which blanketed the

---

[36] https://jewishencyclopedia.com/articles/11761-organ and
https://www.aishdas.org/asp/the-magrefah-and-yiras-hashem
(accessed on 15/04/21)
[37] Angela Curtis, p. 39

vast golden mountain and the translucent Crystal Palace that rose thousands of leagues beyond the white, swirling mists." [38]

The Celestial Temple sits above four golden mountains. In Pesikta de-Rav Kahana 21:4 it is said that God will bring three mountains, Sinai, Tabor, and Carmel, together to build the Temple.

In the book 'Tree of Souls; the Mythology of Judaism' it says of the snow,

"In the beginning, when God desired to create the world, He took snow from beneath the Throne of Glory and cast it into the waters, where it congealed into stone in the midst of the deep. In Sefer ha –Zikhronot 1;6, a midrash reports that the snow came from beneath the Throne of Glory." [39]

"By the breath of God ice is given, and the broad waters are frozen." (Job 37:10)

Enoch's ascension into Heaven is described in *The Book of the Watchers*. This is perhaps the earliest written account of a journey into Heaven, in which Heaven is described as a terrifying place of extremes, of lightning and hailstones, of fire and ice.

The north and the south you created them; Tabor and Hermon joyously praise your name. (Psalm 89:12)

Let's begin with the second half of the verse: "Tabor and Hermon joyously praise your name", a reference to two of the most famous mountains in the Land of Israel. Mount Tabor is

---

[38] Wendy Alec, p. 15
[39] Howard Schwartz, p. 97

located just east of the Nazareth ridge of the Lower Galilee in the Kessuloth branch of the Jezreel Valley. Due to its perfect dome-shaped profile, Mount Tabor is one of the most instantly recognizable mountains in the Land of Israel. Mount Hermon, on the other hand, is a much taller mountain, reaching an elevation of 2814 meters (9232 feet) above sea level, which is the highest peak in the Anti-Lebanon range. Due to its prominent height, Hermon was famously referred to as "the eyes of the country" by an Israeli soldier in the 1973 Yom Kippur War. It is also a very wide mountain (technically a bloc of mountains) which spreads 45 kilometres across the borders of three modern countries: Syria, Lebanon and Israel. Covered in snow much of the year, it is the principle source of the fresh water that runs through the Jordan Rift Valley: into the Sea of Galilee, through the Jordan River and finally into the Dead Sea.[40]

Are there white horses in Heaven?

> *"And I saw **heaven** opened, and behold a **white horse;** and he that sat upon him was called Faithful and True, and in righteousness he doth judge and make war." (Revelation 19:11)*

> *"And the armies of heaven, arrayed in fine linen, white and pure, were following him on white horses. From his mouth comes a sharp sword with which to strike down the nations, and he will rule them with a rod of iron. He will tread the winepress of the fury of the wrath of God the Almighty. ..." (Revelation 19:18)*

---

[40] https://blog.israelbiblicalstudies.com/holy-land-studies/four-sacred-mountains/ (accessed 15/04/21)

The Candle Room
In
Jesus'
Palace

It is interesting to note that in Jesus' palace in Heaven, He has a room that has many different candles. These candles of various sizes represent people's souls (spirits) in the Kingdom. This candle metaphor becomes very clear and intriguing. Many Jewish writings say a candle is the health of a person's soul. Proverbs 20:27 says, '*The spirit of a man is the lamp of the LORD, searching out his inmost being.*'

One child's testimony of the Candle Room,

"The next time I visited Jesus' palace, an angel took me to the third floor where there was a huge room filled with hundreds of bright coloured candles. They were everywhere, on shelves, stands, and tables. There were big fat ones the size of my body and tall skinny ones that reached almost as high as the ceiling. There were candles so small, they looked like Christmas tree lights, and there were three spiral candles that sat in the branches of a giant stand. No matter how long these candles burned, they never dripped wax or melted down. As I walked around, I noticed each candle flame had its own bright, unique colour and scent. Even though there were hundreds of candles in the room, their fragrance didn't overwhelm me. They mingled together instead, creating a scent unlike anything I'd ever smelt before. I spent a lot of time there because it was so peaceful. There were also other people there, worshipping. I watched the burning wicks flicker and paint the floors with shadows that formed the words, Holy, Holy, Holy. Even the candles worship Jesus in heaven." [41]

---

[41] Angela Curtis, p. 36

What is amazing is that this is a child's encounter, and they would not know the depths of the theology that follows. The Candle Room reveals profound revelation of the state of our souls, while we walk out our lives on earth. They represent the health of our spiritual life.

> *"You are the salt of the earth; but if the salt loses its flavour, how shall it be seasoned? It is then good for nothing but to be thrown out and trampled underfoot by men. You are the light of the world. A city that is set on a hill cannot be hidden. Nor do they light a lamp and put it under a basket, but on a lampstand, and it gives light to all who are in the house. Let your light so shine before men, that they may see your good works and glorify your Father in heaven." (Matthew 5:13-16)*

The text says, 'You are the light of the world. A city that is set on a hill cannot be hidden. The City in the "Heavenly Zion" is on a hill. If you are in the City, you bring light, shining in good works and glory. This light is like a candle on lampstands, and in the encounter, the candles worshipped Jesus showing they represent us. If we follow Proverbs 20:27, 'The spirit of a man is the lamp of the LORD, searching out his inmost being.', then these candles are symbolic of people spirits/souls. The City is a house, but the City is not Jesus' Palace, but this Palace, which is large, is found inside the City, close to the Throne.

In the encounter, the candles were in Jesus' Palace and the flickering shadows, spelled out 'Holy, Holy, Holy'. Does this symbolize the Holy of Holies or a sacred place?

Interestingly, those who lose their saltiness, or hide their light, are said to be thrown out, not burnt up, but put out. In its context, this was most likely the earthly city's experience in AD70, in Jerusalem, but it is also pointing to the Heavenly City as well, being put out somewhere in Eden under the trees.

> *"But in a great house, there are not only vessels of gold and silver, but also of wood and clay, some for honour and some for dishonour. Therefore, if anyone cleanses himself from the latter, he will be a vessel for honour, sanctified and useful for the Master, prepared for every good work." (2 Timothy 2:20-21)*

Is there such a place in Jewish thought?

A Jewish talk 'Ha –Ba'al ha Ketanah', says;

> *"The man went deeper and deeper into that forest until, at last, he arrived at a clay hut. Through the window, he saw many flickering flames, and he was curious about them. So, he went to the door and knocked. No answer, he knocked again. Nothing. At last, he pushed the door open and stepped inside. Now, as soon as he stepped inside that cottage, the man realized that it was much larger on the inside than it had seemed to be from the outside. It was filled with hundreds of shelves and on every shelf were dozens of oil candles. Some of those candles were in precious holders of gold or silver or marble, and some were in cheap holders of clay or tin. And some of the holders were filled with oil, and the flames burned brightly, while others had very little oil. All at once, an old man, with a long white beard wearing a white robe, appeared before him, 'Shalom Aleichem, my son,' the old man said. 'How can I help you?' The man replied, 'I have gone everywhere searching for justice, but never have I seen anything like this. Tell me,*

what are all these candles?' The old man said, 'Each of these candles is the candle of a person's soul'." [42]

If this is speaking about our earthly lives, then does it have a spiritual connection above as well? Once saved, we are a lamp which is lit and placed in God's house upon a hill to shine so that people can see our good works and glorify our Father. This house is the City in Eden, for who may ascend to the hill of the Lord, but he who has clean hands and a pure heart? But if we lose our light, we are placed outside the City. We are still saved, but we are hiding our light and good works.

There is another folk tale called 'The Enchanted Inn', in which a boy finds a candle about to burn out and pours additional oil into it as a good deed, only to discover later that it was the candle of his soul.

"The mystery of the seven stars which you saw in My right hand, and the seven golden lampstands. The seven stars are the angels of the seven churches, and the seven lampstands which you saw are the seven churches." (Revelation 1:20)

"Remember therefore from where you have fallen; repent and do the first works, or else I will come to you quickly and remove your lampstand from its place – unless you repent." (Revelation 2:5)

We see clearly in the book of Revelation that 'lampstands' speak of Churches, not Israel, or nonbelievers. To the loveless Church, He says, repent, or I will remove your lampstand. Not I will blow it out, but I will remove it from a place.

---

[42] Howard Schwartz, p. 43

"And to the angel of the church in Sardis write, These things says he who has the seven stars, I know your works, that you have a name that you are alive, but you are dead. Be watchful, and strengthen the things that remain, that are ready to die for I have not found your works perfect before God. Remember therefore how you have received and heard; hold fast and repent. Therefore, I will come upon you as a thief... You have a few names even in Sardis who have not defiled their garments, and they should walk with Me in white, for they are worthy. He who overcomes shall be clothed in white garments, and I will not blot out his name from the Book of Life; but I will confess his name before My Father and before His angels. He who has an ear let him hear what the Spirit says to the churches." (Revelation 3:1-6)

Jesus knows their works, a lot of which is not good, and they are told to strengthen what remains, hold fast, and repent. He says there are few who have not defiled their garments in this dead church, which is spiritually in a bad situation. This garment is not the garment of salvation (justification), this is the garment of sanctification, "And to her, it was granted to be arrayed in fine linen, clean and bright, for the fine linen is the 'righteous acts' (works) of the saints." (Revelation 19:8). The Church of Sardis was not run by 90% non-Christians; they were dead in the sense of not being healthy. Those few who are in a good place will walk with Jesus in His City for they are worthy, prepared, and have yielded to sanctification. To those who overcome their names will not be blotted out from the 'Book of Life'.

Now, no Christian can lose their salvation, so what is the meaning of this text? When we are saved, our names are written into the 'Book of Life', enrolled in the High Calling to rule with Christ. Those who are found worthy enter into roles inside the City. But those who defile their garments, live in gross sin, are unprepared, unsanctified, their names will be blotted out, not removed from existence, still in Heaven, but have a line through their name being disqualified from a placement, as not worthy. Reread the parable of the 10 virgins (Matthew 25:1-13) and the man who came to the wedding banquet with incorrect clothing (Matthew 22:2-14), and read these Scriptures with a new understanding!

The Book of Life is an enrolment book for those worthy to abide in the City. The Book of Life in the secular world was to denote citizenship. The overcomers will have a special entrance by the gates into the City as described in Revelation 22:14.

Joseph Dillow, in his book, 'Final Destiny, The Future Reign of the Servant Kings', says of the Book of Life,

> *"If 'name' in Revelation 3:5 refers to a reputation or title, then God is saying, 'I will not erase his title or reputation from the book of life'. A name in the sense of 'title' or 'reputation' may be blotted out but not in the sense of person. The quality of eternal life is determined by one's faithfulness."* [43]

> *"In the middle of its street, and on either side of the river, was the tree of life, which bore twelve fruits, each tree yielding its fruit every month. The leaves of the tree were for the healing of the nations." (Revelation 22:2)*

---

[43] Joseph Dillow, Final Destiny: The Future Reign of the Servant Kings, Grace Theology Press, 2018, p. 686

"Blessed are those who wash their robes that they may have the right to the tree of life, and may enter through the gates into the city." (Revelation 22:14)

"And the nations of those who are saved shall walk in its light, and the kings of the earth bring their glory and honour into it." (Revelation 21:24)

The *Golden*

Bridge
to the

Throne of

Mercy

We are told to follow the paths of righteousness in Scripture, to follow Jesus because He is the Way, the Truth and the Life, and no man can come to the Fathers throne except through Him. Above the River of Life is a "Golden Bridge", that is the path into the golden gates of the Walls of the City. This pathway also leads into the Fathers gardens, mansions and throne of mercy.

Many who arrive in Heaven get to play on this bridge, and many get to meet love ones who have passed over.

One encounter of Heaven describes it as follows:

> *"The bridge is over 150 feet long; on both ends is a golden road. I met my childhood friend Jerissa in heaven. She died not long ago, I was happy when I saw her smiling and laughing. She has been so sad on earth."* [44]

Now some may say, where is this "Golden Bridge" concept found? Is it even Biblical or even in Jewish thought? The answer is yes, it is in Jewish thought, and even also in Islamic thought! They both hold to a view that when the dead rise, they will be judged to see if they can pass the Golden Bridge. Now, I don't follow the Islamic interpretation, but they still have the concept and most likely got it from the Jewish concept.

Another Child testifies,

> *"One of the children's favourite places to visit in Heaven is the golden bridge. They tell us it glows with light and rises sixty feet above a section of the River of Life. It flows through a beautiful garden. The children like to jump off the golden bridge and dive into the river*

---

[44] Angela Curtis, p. 52

below... Anna said, 'Sometimes we jumped off and floated down the river. We could stand on the water if we wanted to. Other times we floated all the way to a waterfall that doesn't fall down like on earth. It shoots us straight right to the top of the hill... I've seen the River of Life flowing from under the throne.'" [45]

Another reflection,

"As I followed the river up and beyond the waterfall, there was a path winding its way alongside the river. Everything is living, bursting with vibrant energy and emotions, even the paths that you walk on. This path wound through amazing beautiful trees and plants bursting with colours, vibrant beyond earthly reality. As I followed the path, it led to a bridge, but the river continues to another series of waterfalls, all cascading down into a deep pool. When I first discovered this, my focus was on discovering its source, so I went up the nearest waterfall and continued following the river until it came to the tree of life." [46]

Over the bridge one is lead to the Throne of Grace, the Mercy Seat. It seems this "Golden Bridge" is a meeting place for those who arrive in Heaven, and it is also is a place that those who are in right-standing can pass over the bridge to the Throne of mercy and go into the deeper realms of Heaven; into the temple and throne inside the City. It seems some can cross it now, but on judgment day, the unworthy will not be able.

---

[45] Angela Curtis, p. 52

[46] Mike Parsons, My Journey Beyond Beyond, The Choir Press Publishers, 2018, p. 98

Reflections and conclusions,

- In Heaven, there is a Golden Bridge over the River of Life that leads to the Throne of Mercy and into the Temple and City in Eden.

- In Jewish thought, and one must understand that they make up expressions of truth (stretch truth at times), that there is a bridge over Gehenna. Here, the spirits of the dead are forced to cross a bridge that seems to be very narrow, losing their balance, they fall off into the abyss. The point is that those who have not walked the narrow path (Jesus spoke of) on judgement day, will have nothing to depend on and won't be able to pass over. I would say they don't even get near the bridge, as the dead (nonbelievers) are judged at the "Great White Throne" and don't walk to the Throne of Grace or Mercy Seat. Either way, with the limited revelation they had, they knew of a bridge. (Sedar Eliyahu Zuta 21,76b; B.Ervin 19a, B. Sukkah 32B)

- Islamic thought, which I do not follow, holds that the last phase of judgement is the crossing of the 'Sirat or Seerat', the bridge over Hell. The Quran's references to this bridge are rather obscure (36:66; 37:23-24).

- My thoughts are: From listening to and reading the Heaven encounters who have seen this bridge in Eden, I don't believe that the bridge is hanging over Hell. But I would say it is a place of arrival, and a place of judgement. It will be used as the pathway of righteousness to give an account – those who believe will pass over to the Mercy Seat, Throne of Grace, and our works will be judged by fire, and then we will move on. Others will not pass over the bridge; they will not have walked the narrow path and unbelievers will be judged at the Great White Throne (then cast into Hell).

As Above, so below:

The Gate of Mercy in the Eastern Wall is an ancient structure in Jerusalem that is both part of the Eastern side of the city wall of Jerusalem and the Eastern wall of the ancient Temple Mount. The Jewish belief is that this is the location (valley of Jehoshaphat) where the dead will be raised first.

Muslim scholars talk about the Sirat Bridge Marker or Pillar that is a small protruding pillar close to the Southern edge of the Temple Mount's eastern wall. This pillar marks the location of the Sirat bridge. According to Islamic tradition, this is the location where one end of the Sirat bridge will be hung over Jahannam. It is called in Islamic thought the Armchair or Seat of Muhammad. The bridge will begin at the Eastern wall of the Temple Mount and will end on the Mount of Olives. Not that we follow the Islamic teachings, but it is interesting that they also believe that, on the day of judgment, all people will have to walk across a bridge to see who has followed the path of righteousness. So, the idea of a bridge in Heaven is not new. (My refinement would be, not all people will walk across it)

Conclusions, and not being too dogmatic, I think we can say there is a thought in Jewish and Islamic thought, a bridge leads into the gates into the Temple Mount. And their belief is that on the Day of Judgment in Heaven, some will pass across to the Throne of Grace, Mercy Seat, and enter the City, others will not. The idea of a bridge is Biblical and also testified from Heaven encounters. The bridge is a very large bridge and leads to the Tree of Life, which is in the Heavenly City. The streets of gold are in the city, and the road leading over the bridge also seems to be gold. Are bridges in Heaven? I think we can conclude YES!

Ian Clayton says of the golden bridge,

> *"I knew the river was the key because when you follow the river, it leads through your garden, up this glorious waterfall into Eden, which is His garden. I did not know that you could swim up river, you could float up river, you could fly up river, you could anything you like up the river. I did not know that, so I figured I would jump into the river and just start walking because there is no resistance in the river, and it's not hard work. When I got in, I started to float up the waterfall."* [47]

> *"It came to the point where I knew I had to go and encounter Jesus. There is a pathway that runs along the river, and then there is a bridge. I could see Jesus looking at the bridge."* [48]

---

[47] Ian Clayton, The Realms of the Kingdom, Volume One, Seraph Creative Publishing, 2014, p. 98
[48] Ian Clayton, p. 99

Eagles
of
Revelation,
Protection
and Restoration

The children report on their visits to Heaven of an area where hundreds of eagles are in training for the Lord. The Scriptures give us several passages about Eagles. Many of us interpret them as being symbolic only, but I believe a deeper truth is that they are spiritually real.

One person's testimony,

> *"There are huge eagles in Heaven. They're amazing. I got to fly on one. It took me and the Holy Spirit to a special place where there were hundreds of eagles. What are they doing? I asked. They are training for the Lord's service, He said. Then our eagle flew above a vast area where we watched them learn to fly, dive and manoeuvre and different obstacles."* [49]

Eagles in Heaven?

The eagles in Heaven train for new seasons to empower the body of Christ. When they are released for assignments, they fly in spirit imparting new revelation to seers and protecting young ones in the faith. With the angels, they also release healing and strength.

They are a manifestation of seeing the big picture and giving sharp insight into the unfolding Kingdom. The airborne eagles represent God, and the grounded, moulting eagles represent us. Eagles go through seasons of renewing their feathers and strength, and like us, we must feed off God, and renew our strength under His wings. The wings of these trained eagles carry

---

[49] Angela Curtis, p. 125

the presence of God and impart restoration, renewed strength and revelation.

> *"But those who hope in the Lord will renew their strength. They will soar on wings of eagles; they will run and not grow weary; they will walk and not be faint." (Isaiah 40:31)*

> *"Give praise to the Lord, O my soul; let not all his blessings go from your memory. He has forgiveness for all sin, He takes away all your diseases, He keeps back your life from destruction, crowning you with mercy and grace. He makes your mouth full of good things, so that your strength is made new again like the eagles." (Psalms 103:2-5)*

Eagles protect, guard, train and deliver:

> *"You have seen what I did to the Egyptians and how I bore you on eagle's wings and brought you to Myself. Now therefore, if you will obey My voice in truth and keep My covenant, then you shall be My own peculiar possession and treasure from among and above all people; for all the earth is Mine. And you shall be to Me a kingdom of priests, a holy nation. Set apart to the worship of God." (Exodus 19:4-6)*

> *"For the Lord's portion is His people, Jacob is the allotment of His inheritance. He found him in a desert land, and in the howling waste of a wilderness; He encircled him, He cared for him, He guarded him as the pupil of its young. Like an eagle that stirs up its nest, that hovers over its young, he spread His wings and caught them, He carried them on His pinions. The Lord*

alone guided him, and there was no foreign god with him." (Deuteronomy 32:9-12)

As we become strong trees planted with our spirits and hearts set on things in Heaven, growing by the river, the eagles of Heaven come down and rest on our lives on earth for the impartation of restoration, renewed strength, discernment, revelation and wisdom.

> *"For as the earth brings forth its bud, As the garden causes the things that are sown in it to spring forth, So the Lord will cause righteousness and praise to spring forth before all nations." (Isaiah 61:11)*

Wendy Alec describes,

> *"Now, amongst the beauty that was now arising all over the vast expanse, I saw two large trees that had grown seemingly out of nowhere and towered over the garden. In fact, now that I looked, these trees were appearing on the surrounding edge of the garden. These, I sensed, represented apostolic works in the earth today – that had already provided much sustenance for the Lord's people, and he was well pleased. But I saw that in this season, there was to be a different mandate and an even wider influence because they had proven trustworthy in the past season. As I looked at the trees in front of me, I saw huge branches start to grow from the trunks and roots go down hundreds of feet below the surface, and suddenly, many eagles, previously unseen, stirred as one. Magnificent white and golden eagles flew from the branches. I felt that because of the strength and sturdiness and expanse of their reach, the trees were Apostolic, representing the structure developers and the*

builders. The eagles, these were the Prophets and Seers. These were the Apostolic and Prophetic works that were rising in the earth. " [50]

"Outside the Palace, the outer brilliance of the radiance emanated from thousands of translucent, angelic forms and white eagles, which blanketed the vast golden mountains... " [51]

---

[50] Wendy Alec, *Visions of Heaven*, Warboys Publishers, 2013, p. 79
[51] Wendy Alec, The Fall of Lucifer, Warboys Publishers, 2008, p. 16

Weeping on the Rocks in the Shadows of Eden

We now come to one of the most puzzling and not often talked about areas in Heaven. Many would wish it didn't exist, but it does, and we must walk carefully in life pursuing our High Calling.

During one of the weeks I was there, the children would come back from their visions (worship/prayer times) and share where Jesus had taken them. This week was unusual, they spoke about Jesus taking them to an area in Heaven that was dim, and the light was grey. They said it was not like the rest of Heaven, being bright with colour and great light. This place was kind of dark and far from the light of the City. Each day they would come back and share more. One time, they took fruit from the garden (Revelation 22:2) to feed the people there. These people weren't in torment, but they weren't that happy. What was this place? I kept asking myself.

> *"As the week passed, we learnt that this small area is outside the City, outside of the reach of the light of the City at some distance. The people there, who are believers, look skinny with plain clothes, no beautiful garments on like the rest in Heaven. There were a few houses, and they looked like little huts down in the forest land. Some people were praising God by the rocks of a stream and others were weeping. You may be thinking, is this place Hell? No, it is in Heaven, and those there are in the Kingdom, but have lived extremely carnal and abusive lives as believers."* [52]

Their clothing, their skinny bodies reveal their spiritual maturity and lack of growth in sanctification.

---

[52] My personal conversations with those who were involved in receiving this revelation.

One of the adults that has also been taken to see this area, shared that this place is *not* Hell. It is a place for carnal believers, gross living, and for those who damage others spiritually. They are there in a place of remorse (weeping and gnashing of teeth) to untangle soul issues. They are saved, but they are not prepared or sanctified to a degree to go further. This adult had personally seen a person they knew there! Those there wonder and think under the trees, and Jesus at times goes down to visit them. On their birthdays (spiritual – the day they accepted Christ as Saviour), they are brought up to the City to celebrate with others. The way we live truly matters, and how we live has consequences.

> *"And whatever you do, do it heartily as to the Lord and not to men, knowing that from the Lord you will receive the reward of inheritance; for you serve the Lord Christ. But he who does wrong will be repaid for what he has done. And there is no partiality." (Colossians 3:23-25)*

The Church Father Irenaeus, writing in AD180, said,

> *"It was not to those who are on the outside that he said these things, but to us – lest we should be cast forth from the kingdom of God, by doing any such thing."*

The definition of 'cast forth' is, "to throw out, or eject, as from an enclosed place, to emit, to send out." It is to be sent out from the light and entrance of the Heavenly City to lower regions of the Kingdom in Eden. Scripture calls this place 'Outer Darkness', where there will be weeping and gnashing of teeth. They are saved, in Heaven, in the Kingdom, but sent out to the darkness outside the light of God's city, for a time to be restored. There is a difference between the darkness outside, due to the distance from the lighted City in Paradise (Revelation 21:23), "the blackness of darkness forever" in Jude 1:13, and the Lake of Fire (Revelation 20:10).

When Adam and Eve sinned, they were cast out of the garden in Paradise, outside the light of God's glory and into outer darkness.

> *Irenaeus, AD180, said, "And God planted a garden eastward in Eden, and there He placed man whom He had formed. And then afterwards, when man proved disobedient, he was cast out from there into the world."*

In Heaven, there is no sun, only the light of God's glory in His city. Believers who have been unfaithful, and therefore don't wear the wedding garments (righteous acts of the saints – Revelation 19:8), will be "cast into outer darkness" and not be allowed into the Wedding Banquet or Marriage Supper of the Lamb. They will knock and ask to come in (Luke 13:25), but they will be taken to a region that is outside the City light's radiance, where the land is dim and grey. They will stay there until they have untangled soul issues and dealt with unforgiveness, and restoration has come to those who were abused. Over time, there will be a shift from Heaven to earth through many people's prayers (including the one untangling their issues) that brings freedom to the abused one while they live on earth. Once the issues have been dealt with, the restored 'unfaithfuls' will make their way into the City, but for now, they are unprepared.

We are saved by the righteousness of Jesus and forgiven of all our sins. And from this, we are translated into the Kingdom of light out of the Kingdom of darkness. We are eternally saved, but we must walk out our sanctification and put on the garments of transforming glory by living a life of righteous acts.

"But if you refuse to forgive others, your Father will not forgive your sins." (Matthew 6:15)

"If you forgive the sins of any, they are forgiven; if you retain the sins of any, they are retained." (John 20:23).

"Therefore, we also, since we are surrounded by so great a cloud of witnesses, let us lay aside every weight, and sin which so easily entangles us, and let us the run with endurance the race that is set before us." (Hebrews 12:1)

"And now, little children, abide in Him, that when He appears, we may have confidence and not shrink back ashamed before Him at His coming." (John 2:28)

"He who says he is in the light, and hates his brother, is in darkness until now. He who loves his brother abides in the light, and there is no cause for stumbling in him. But he who hates his brother is in darkness and walks in darkness, and does not know where he is going, because the darkness has blinded his eyes." (John 2:9-11)

The *Darkness*
outside
the
Palace
- References

When it comes to passages in Scripture concerning the darkness outside, or 'Outer Darkness', as many translate it - there are three main places in the Gospels where the term is used. The term 'Outer Darkness' appears three times in Scripture, and always to do with the Kingdom of Heaven, and 'being cast out', and with 'weeping and gnashing of teeth' (Matthew 8:12; Matthew 22:13; Matthew 25:30).

In interpreting these terms, we must be aware there are different types of 'darkness' in Scripture,

- The key phrase in Greek is *'skotos to exoteron'*, simply translated 'the darkness outside'. If there is anything to be made of the word order, it would be that the adjective "outside" is specifying either the kind or the location of the darkness. Banquets in the Middle East were held at night. So in saying this, those outside the lighted city/palace/hall are not in hell, they are simply outside the building where the light (glory of God is bright inside) is.[53]

- The three places that the term 'the darkness outside' or 'outer darkness' is used, the word hell, fire, or furnace are never mentioned in the same context or passage.

- Jude 1:13 – blackness of darkness forever, and 2 Peter 2:4 – hell, darkness, blackness forever, judgment - is not the same darkness which is a backdrop to a lighted place of which one can go in and out.

You must be in the Feast before you can be cast out of it!

---

[53] Joseph Dillow, *Final Destiny: The Future Reign of the Servant Kings*, Grace Theology Press, 2018, p. 789

- But the sons of the Kingdom will be thrown out into the darkness (Matthew 8:12). Those in Israel who had little faith and fell in disobedience will be cast out – Unfaithful covenant believers.

- Parable of the Weeds (Matthew 13:24-30; 37-43). The good seed stands for the sons of the Kingdom, believers, whether carnal or faithful. The Tares are unbelievers, sons of the evil one (devil) will be cast into the furnace (Hell).

- Parable of the Wedding Banquet (Matthew 22:13). At the end of the age, Believers in the Kingdom will either enter the banquet or be left outside but still be in the Kingdom (Heaven). Those who will be cast out into another region into darkness, (but not hell) are carnal, unworthy, faithless believers. Only those who are prepared and have dressed themselves in the garment of the 'righteous acts' of the saints will be allowed to enter, that being the faithful. Those led outside, are those who walked consistently carnal and have defiled their garments (Revelation 3:4) and shown the shame of their nakedness (Revelation 3:18).

- Parable of the Ten Virgins (Matthew 25:10). They all had 'oil', were regenerated (believers), but only five prepared themselves; the other five were lazy, unfaithful, and carnal. The five who were prepared were faithful overcomers.

- Parable of the Talents (Matthew 25:25,29). The worthless servant was thrown into the darkness (not hell, not the fire, or furnace, but outside the light of the city/palace).

Scriptures to focus on,

"Then the King said to the servants, Bind him hand and foot, take him away, and cast him into outer darkness, there will be weeping and gnashing of teeth." *(Matthew 22:13)*

"Anyone who claims to be in the light but hates his brother is still in the darkness. Whoever loves his brother lives in the light, and there is nothing in him to make him stumble. But whoever hates his brother is in darkness and walks around in darkness; he does not know where he is going, because the darkness has blinded him." (1 John 2:9-11)

Interpreters and Quotes,

2 Enoch 42:1-5, "And I saw the key-holders and the guards of hell standing as large as serpents, with their face like lamps that have been extinguished, and their eyes aflame, and their teeth naked down to their breasts. And I said to their faces, "It would have been better if I had not seen you, nor heard about your activities, nor that any member of my tribe had been brought to you. To what small extent they have sinned in this life, but eternal life they will suffer forever. AND – I ascended to the east into the paradise of Eden, where rest is prepared for the righteous. And it is open as far as the 3rd heaven; but it is closed off from the world. And the guards are appointed at the very large gates of the east of the sun, angels of flame, singing victory songs, never silent, rejoicing at the arrival of the righteous. When the last one arrives, he will bring out Adam, together with the ancestors; and he will bring them in there, so that they may be filled with joy, just as a person invites his best friends to have dinner with him and they arrive with joy, and they talk together in front of that man's palace, waiting with joyful anticipation to have dinner with delightful enjoyments and riches that cannot be measured, and joy and happiness in eternal light and life."

Enoch makes it clear that there are saved people waiting in Paradise for a special dinner. If this dinner is taking place at night, then the darkness outside the Palace is not hell. Two different gates are present, one gate for hell, and another gate for Paradise. Enoch ascends from the gates of hell to the gates of paradise. The gates of Paradise are closed off from the gates of hell and separated by his lengthy ascension. Enoch pictures the place outside the palace to be a place of joyful anticipation of the dinner. If one were to be 'cast back' into this place after the dinner has started (which is the case in Matthew's Gospel), they would not be cast into the fire. Before dinner, those outside the front of the palace were not in fire, neither are they in this identical place *after* dinner. The darkness outside the front of the palace is not a place of fire.[54]

Jesus adds that the outer darkness is a buffer zone between the outside of the palace and the darkness of hell. The buffer zone is inside of Paradise, far removed from the gates of hell (Is NOT HELL). To be in darkness, outside the palace, is to be within the gates of Paradise. Being cast out into the Biblical outer darkness is to be cast outside of the King's Palace, not outside of the King's Kingdom. The outer darkness is a place for unfaithful believers who have not washed their robes and walked worthy.

---

[54] Marty Cauley, *The Outer Darkness: Its interpretations and Implications*, Misthological Press, 2012, p. 475

They are placed outside in a dim area of Paradise, away from the light of the great city and palace to 'out-work heart issues.

Let's recap the description of Heaven here: The throne is at the top of the City, in the temple complex or sanctuary, and the river runs down through the street. The throne area is a large segment, away from people's mansions. Close to the throne is Jesus' Palace in the City. The Golden Bridge connects an entrance into the City to the Throne. The throne area is upon a hill, and somewhat down the hill, there is a path that goes underground, beneath the throne to the Father's Garden and Pool of Tears. Unfaithful believers are judged at the throne, unable to enter the Palace, and are then led outside the City to the shadow area of Eden.

God is light, and in Him, there is no darkness. When Adam and Eve were banished from the Garden of Eden, they were sent out into darkness. They walked in darkness and wandered outside the Garden. They were in Eden but driven to the east of Eden. (Genesis 1:1-5)

> *"Do you not know that those who run in a race all run, but one receives the prize. Run in such a way that you may obtain it. And everyone who competes for the prize is temperate in all things. Now they do it to obtain a perishable crown, but we for an imperishable crown. Therefore, I run thus, not with uncertainty. Thus I fight; not as one who beats the air. But I discipline my body and bring it into subjection lest, when I have preached to others, I myself should become a castaway."*
> *(1 Corinthians 9:24-27)*

The Shepherd of Hermas AD100-200,

"The stones which are rejected but not cast away are sinners who may yet become part of the tower if they repent; however, they must repent before the tower (city) is complete. Hermas asks the matron if repentance is possible for those who have been cast away. The answer is that it is possible, but they will not have a place in this tower. Instead, they will dwell in an inferior place (outer darkness) for a time." (Hermas AD100-200)

"As the presbyters say, those who are deemed worthy of an abode in heaven will go there, others will enjoy the delights of Paradise, and others will possess the splendour of the city. For everywhere, the Saviour will be seen, depending on the worthiness of those who see him. There is a distinction between the habitation of those who produce a hundredfold, those who produce sixty-fold, and those who produce thirtyfold. For the first will be taken up into the heavens, the second will dwell in Paradise, and the last will inhabit the city. It was on this account the Lord said, "In My Father's house are many mansions." The presbyters, the disciples of the apostles, affirmed this is the graduation and arrangement of those who are saved, and that they advance through steps of this nature." (Papias, AD120)

"There are various abodes according to the worth of those who have believed." (Clement of Alexandria, AD195)

"The Lord says 'And other sheep there are also not of this fold', These are deemed worthy of another fold and mansion." (Clement of Alexandria, AD195)

"The Lord does not profess to give the same honours to all. Rather, to some, He promises that they will be numbered in the Kingdom of Heaven. To others, they are promised the inheritance of the earth. And still others, there is promised the privilege to see the Father." (Methodius, AD290)

The Church Father Ephrem of Nisibis, AD300, wrote,

"the foothills of Paradise the very outer slopes of the Mountain of Paradise wherein penitents would dwell, a place of lessor honour but nonetheless of salvation. Those who have heard the Word but are on the fringes of the Church, apparently have some hope of salvation after enduring a period of chastisement."

In Olshausen's first German commentary of Matthew 25:14-30, in which he concluded that verse 30 describes believers who are cast into outer darkness, but not into fire, he says the following:

"The immediate reference is not to eternal condemnation, but to exclusion from where the faithful enter. The degree of guilt, in the case of the unfaithful, determines the possibility of their awakened repentance. The kingdom is finally viewed as a region of light encircled by darkness. And in reference to this point, the metaphorical language of Scripture is very exact in the choice of expressions. Concerning the children of light who are unfaithful to their vocation, it is said that they are cast into the darkness; but the children of darkness,

we are told that they are consigned to everlasting fire."
[55]

"In 1863, Dean Alford wrote in his Greek Testament commentary, "the outer darkness refers to the exclusion of unfaithful believers from the marriage supper, but that they were still in the Kingdom. To be cast out into outer darkness means to be outside the lighted chamber of the feast." [56]

Thayer's Greek/English Lexicon says that the outer darkness is "the darkness outside the limits of the lighted palace". It's evidentially a space in the Kingdom, but outside the circle of men and women whose faithfulness earned them a special rank.

The NIBC, with its corresponding Nelson Study Bible, says that the "outer darkness" is a reward issue, not a hell issue.

G.H. Lang — *"Being sent out to the garden outside the banquet hall is a completely different destiny from that of the tares, the sons of the evil one (Matthew 13:38), being cast into the furnace of fire, eternal damnation, where there will also be wailing and gnashing of teeth."*

Recent Scholars:

Dr. Marty Cauley, in his book, Outer Darkness: Its Interpretations and Implications, says, *"it is outside the City in Eden, and is not hell. There is a difference between the darkness outside the light of the City (Rev 21:23), and Jude 1:12, 'the blackness of darkness forever' (which is hell)."*

---

[55] Marty Cauley, p. 456
[56] Marty Cauley, p. 454

Dr. Spiros Zodhiates – The Complete Word Study New Testament, says, *"the outer darkness, and weeping and gnashing of teeth are terms that may be applied to believers who have failed the Lord in their service. In the instance, the outer darkness may be a reference to a place or a position of far less rewards for the servants who proved themselves less diligent than those who used and exercised their talents to the fullest."* [57]

Dr. Kenneth Wuest – Greek New Testament says, *"this darkness is simply the darkness that is outside the Kings banqueting house. It is not hell."* [58]

Dr. Michael Huber – Dallas Theological Seminary – The concept of the Outer Darkness – *"It is related to outside the Temple".*[59]

Dr. Charles Stanley – Eternal Security book says, *"to be in the outer darkness is to be in the kingdom of God but outside the circle of men and women whose faithfulness on this earth earned them a special rank or position. The outer darkness here simply refers to being thrown outside a building; it is not a description of hell."* [60]

"Dr Tony Evens says, "The outer darkness described in this passage is not a description of hell, but is likely a lessor status in God's kingdom. Unfaithful Christians will see more diligent Christians rule and reign with Christ. Realizing that they could have had much greater reward and

---

[57] As cited in Chuck Missler, *The Kingdom, Power & Glory*, The Kings High Way Publishers, 2007, p. 62
[58] As cited by Chuck Missler, p. 89
[59] As cited by Chuck Missler, p. 146

[60] Charles Stanley, *Eternal Security: Can you be sure?* (1990) As cited in Dennis Rosker, Should Christians Fear Outer Darkness, Grace Gospel Press, 2015, p. 20

prominence in God's kingdom, these unfaithful stewards will weep and gnash in deep remorse and regret."[61]

Dr. Bob Wilkin of the Grace Evangelical Society says the outer darkness is outside the banqueting house in the Kingdom, it is not hell.

Chuck Missler in his book, The Kingdom, Power & Glory, says, *"Outer Darkness – This does not speak of hell. Nor is it a place where unbelievers go (1 John 2:9-11). It's the place where the unfaithful and disobedient believers will dwell during the Millennium while they learn sanctification. It's a separate place, another room or region outside of the light of the presence of the Lord. The outer darkness is the darkness outside the limits of the lighted palace."* [62]

Dr. Jospeh Dillow, in his book, The Reign of the Servant Kings, says, *"The notions of heaven or hell are simply not part of the semantic value of the words. The fact that the nonbeliever can experience profound regret in hell in no way implies that the true Christian cannot experience profound regret in the kingdom (there will be remorse in heaven). It seems that those verses are regret for the unfaithful Christian which Matthew's mentions 'wailing and gnashing of teeth.' Outer darkness is a time of rebuke, regret, reflection, and repentance. The furnace of fire which is a reference to damnation, is used only twice and never in association with the darkness outside"* [63]

Dillow continues, *"Matthew, therefore, leads us to imagine a feast of great rejoicing. All the faithful Christians of the Church are there to celebrate*

[61] Tony Evans, *Rewards for Christians in the Tim La Haye Prophecy Study Bible* (2000) As cited by Dennis Rosker, p. 20

[62] Chuck Missler, *The Kingdom, Power & Glory*, p. 361

[63] As cited by Dennis Rosker, p. 17

their wedding feast with their King. This joyful banquet is portrayed by the Lord as occurring in the evening in a brightly lit banquet hall. Outside the banquet, where the shining lights of the feast are not present."

The City, the Palace, shines like the sun with the Glory of God. Outside the City, the further away you go, the light is dimmer. This area is the darkness outside the light of the City.

Dr. Zane Hodges, Grace Evangelical Society, says, *"There will be weeping and gnashing of teeth. And well there might be. The unfaithful Christian, like the ill-dressed guest, has missed the wedding supper just as surely as did those who spurned the invitation to begin with. Thus he joins the crowed ranks of many who are called to co-heirship."*

A.B. Badger, Th.M, Th.D., - *"Outer Darkness is not hell".*

Christian Mystic Peter Tan, writes – *"A great number of Christians of the lowest category (1 Corinthians 3:15) are found in this realm. Many of them who have lived worldly and materialistic, unholy and selfish lives remain in the lowest of the earth spheres. The love of the Father is not fully developed in their lives (1 John 2:15). They were surprised at the dimness of light that greeted them. When a spirit departs from the physical body at death, it remains at the same spiritual level as it was when it died. There is no instantaneous super spiritual growth. The character the spirit had while in the physical body is the same character it retains when it leaves the body."* [64]

One of the first real Heaven encounter books to be written, is called, 40 days in Heaven: The True Testimony of Seneca

---

[64] Peter Tan, http://www.greatgenius.com/different-spheres-of-the-spiritual-world, accessed 17/04/2021

Sodi's Visitation to Paradise, the Holy City and the Glory of God's Throne, (1909). Seneca tells us,

"The Light toward the City which I had seen on my first arrival grew more and more glorious as we neared the City. We could at length see the shining of the jasper wall. You see that great Judean gate over there? Its frame and hinges are of the purest gold and set with one great pearl. This gate always stands open, for there is no restraint in heaven. Unbound liberty is now yours forever. And the wall has respect to those outside as well as to those inside. The angel at the gateway is to give direction to all who may inquire. You will further remember that there are twelve of these gates as well as twelve foundations, and there are twelve angels as well as twelve gates. No one can enter these gates not fully prepared. Did you notice some who dropped back far into the rear? In the world, the truth had to be observed for any advancement. This wall with its gates marks definite experience in the journey of the redeemed. It is a fuller development of the great truths suggested by the ancient tabernacle; the holy and the most holy place has reference to the saints on earth and those in heaven. Surely, said the elder, when you are prepared for the light and glory of the city, you will be brought to its gates and ushered in with the welcome of your Lord. If you wait among the trees, do not be restless nor neglectful. Almost the entire catalogue of the Christian graces must be learned by you (on earth, or in heaven – outside the city). Partake freely of the twelve kinds of fruit on the trees, they will impart light, life and grace to your soul. Press the leaves to your nostrils and bind

them to your heart and no taint of evil will remain in you." [65]

Inside the Gates of Heaven by Oden Hetrick, another Heaven encounter book, says,

> *"So also, as we approach God's abode in the sky, we come first to the large Outer Court or suburbs, then to the Holy Place, then to the Most Holy Place where God sits on His Throne. Now, these suburbs of the City of Heaven are very much like earth, with grass, flowers, trees, shadows, birds and animals. This is the place where spiritual principles must be learned by those saints who on earth did not become very spiritually-minded. It is not true that we suddenly know everything when we get to Heaven. Christians on earth are admonished by Scripture.* Study to show yourself approved of God. — *2 Timothy 2:15."* [66]

---

[65] Elwood Scott, *40 Days in Heaven*, First Fruits offering, 2008, p. 36
[66] Oden Hetrick, *Inside the gates of Heaven*, Advanced Global Publishing, 2014.

No Instant
Reset
of
One's Character

Many believe that once they get to Heaven, they will instantly be perfected. They will wake up, and everyone will be fully perfected clones in knowledge and character; that it doesn't really matter how one lives now, just as long as they get to Heaven. Well, it does matter how you live now and how much you yield into sanctification by God's Spirit. We are called to be a living holy sacrifice unto God. There is no instant reset of one's character in Heaven. For what would anyone gain or learn by all being clones? There are gains, and there are losses; there are the faithful and the unfaithful. There are rewards, and there are different regions of light. We arrive in the measure that we have yielded to God's Spirit on earth and prepared ourselves, and we will continue to grow in Heaven for eternity. Jesus was perfected by being tested, tempted, and through his sufferings. It matters how you live on earth!

Let's look at some examples:

Aborted babies or naturally caused deaths of a foetus. Do these people turn up in Heaven as perfect, perfected in character, all-knowing, to the highest degree of glory, as glorified beings? I think not, for would they even know who they were, and what would they have grown or learnt in transformation? I would say these souls turn up in Heaven and are looked after by nurturers and are sent to nurseries and schools, where these young souls grow and mature.

A child – If a child arrives in Heaven as an instant adult, what would the child have learnt; how could they have been perfected or overcome anything? Could they understand the knowledge of being an adult? From the accounts of those who have experienced Heaven, I would say there is growth in Heaven, and these children go to school and graduate from Heaven's Universities.

An unfaithful adult - turns up in Heaven instantly perfect in character, in the highest degree of glory, fully rewarded, same rewards as a faithful believer. If this was so, it would be very unfair, and what has the person learnt in being instantly transformed into the image of the Son, without going from glory to glory?

I believe that being set free from corruption, being sanctified and glorified, means a lot more than an "instant" experience of waking up in Heaven in that state. Yes, there will be some changes and heightened senses and understanding. But I believe for salvation to come to completion, there must be a journey of definite growth and transformation of one's character.

There will be no corruption of body – meaning one cannot die or fall away from God once in Heaven, for His Spirit lives in them.

Sanctification – means one's yielding on earth transform's one's growth, maturity and holiness. And this growth will continue in Heaven at a heightened consciousness for eternity.

Glorification does not mean that we wake up in perfection of knowledge and character in a flash! But that one arrives in Heaven free from death and will go from one glory to another glory – It is not a static state, but a 'growing glory' of an eternal life. Our bodies will be glorified like Jesus and will be able to move as He did after His resurrection.

We have read that there are different areas of Heaven, and the measure of the light you carry (that which has been transformed in you) is the access you have to parts of the Kingdom. As we read in the last Chapter, some very unfaithful adults will go to outer darkness to untangle soul issues.

Some may raise the question, 'How can someone be in Heaven with sin issues? How can sin be there?'

My response is that in many areas of Heaven, sin won't be around because many will have reached a maturity of sanctification. As for the region of 'outer darkness', these people will not continue to sin but will be working out the consequences of their unconfessed (undealt with) sins, which led to their stagnant growth on earth.

Lucifer walked in Heaven with wrong intentions in his heart – this did not get him kicked out until he acted on them. Those in the lowest measure of light (grey area – outer darkness) won't be sinning or acting out sin. They will be freed to a place of remorse (weeping) to untangle wrong intentions in their DNA – carnal strongholds. Once this is done, they will continue in growth and fulfil their irrevocable calling to perfection.

Lucifer walked around Heaven for a long time with wrong intentions. In his glorified state in the garden, Adam must have had a bad thought before he acted and fell from grace. This shows that a glorified state can hold wrong thinking. There is a difference between "desire" and "conceived".

"But each one is tempted when he is drawn away by his own desires and enticed. Then, when desire has conceived, it gives birth to sin; and sin, when it is fully grown, brings forth death." (James 1:14-15)

Those who were unfaithful believers and lack sanctification, will have knowledge of their past sinful intentions and desires. These sinful desires that are/were in them will leave them in remorse, after the experience of the Bema Seat (judgement). They will lack growth and maturity of character, their thoughts and desires will still be in them to be untangled, but they won't have a place to "conceive" them and bring them to birth. They will have God's Spirit in them, and they will not be influenced by the world or the devil and his demons. The atmosphere may be dim in some areas but peaceful. Sin will not be able to be fully grown. But, still, Outer darkness is not the place we would desire to be. Far better to enter the City and dwell in the mansions of God, and explore Eden, and worship at the throne.

When it comes to the terms 'weeping and gnashing of teeth' in correlation to the 'outer darkness' area, some say, 'but doesn't the Bible say, God will wipe away all our tears in Heaven, so there will be no weeping in Heaven?' But the text does not say there are no tears in Heaven.

> *"And God will wipe away every tear from their eyes, there will be no more sorrow, nor crying. There will be no more pain, for the former things have passed away." (Revelation 21:4)*

Jesus is certainly not wiping the eyes of those in Hell in this verse, so He must be wiping people's tears in Heaven. The answer is not that there are no tears in Heaven, but at what stage or locations will there be no tears.

I would say there are at least four times of weeping in Heaven,

1. When all believers appear before the Judgement seat of Christ, and our wounds, sorrows and motives are addressed and rewarded, and many enter the City.

2. When unfaithful, carnal believers are (will be) sent out in their defiled (unsanctified) garments into "outer darkness" in remorse.

3. When Jesus weeps in the present, in Heaven, when He sits by the 'pool of tears' and sees all our tears there, and adds His.

4. When people newly arrive in Heaven and meet family members or old friends, they laugh and cry tears of joy.

Those who walk worthy of their calling will enter Heaven, their tears will be wiped away, and they shall have no more sorrows or hurts and live in bliss. There is no more destructive pain or sorrow.

The

Shepherd

of Hermas:

Stones of the

Tower

An important second-century Christian text read heavily in the early Church was *The Shepherd of Hermas*. Hermas is given these visions both for his own repentance and for sharing the teachings with others. He is urged to forgive his family for the wrongs they have done him so that their sins may be cleansed, "For the remembrance of wrongs worketh death." Many times, the angel warns against the recollection of offences, whether one's own or those of others: "Do not trample (the Lord's) mercy underfoot," he says, "but rather honour Him, because He is so patient with your sins, and is not as you are."

Hermas is given a Vision of the Tower built upon the waters; the City,

"Of the visions shown to Hermas by the matron, the most important is that of a tower being built upon the waters. The tower represents the Church which is built upon the waters of baptism. It is being built by six young men (angels), and other men (lesser angels) are carrying stones out of the water and from the land to be put into the tower.

Stones dragged from the depths of the water are placed in the building as they are because they are already polished and fit perfectly so that the building appears to be made of one stone. These stones are those who have suffered for the Lord's sake. There are white square stones which also fit perfectly; these are apostles, bishops, teachers and deacons, and faithful believers who have served God with purity and lived at peace with one another.

Of the stones taken from the earth, some are rejected while others are fitted into the building; some stones are even cut down from the building itself and cast away. Other stones lie around the building unused because they are rough, have cracks, or are the wrong shape or size.

The stones which are rejected but not cast far away are sinners who may yet become part of the tower if they repent; however, they must repent before the building is finished and there is no longer any room. The stones cut down and thrown far away are evil people, while the many stones lying around unused because of various defects, are those who know the truth and do not remain in it, or have other sins.

There are still more types of stones symbolizing different kinds of people. For example, the stones that are white and round and do not fit are rich men who have true faith but deny the Lord when tribulation comes because of their riches; their riches will need to be shorn away before they can be useful to God.

Hermas asks the matron if repentance is possible for those who have been cast away. The answer is that it is possible, but they will not have a place in this tower. Instead, they will dwell in an inferior place, and only after suffering and having "completed the days of their sins." They must deal with their sins before the Tower is complete; if they do, they can come in. "[67]

---

[67] https://www.newadvent.org/fathers/02011.htm

In the vision above, being his third vision, Hermas met the woman in a field. She was accompanied by six men (angels) who soon left to build a tower of stones upon the water. New stones were added to the tower seamlessly so that it looked as though it was one stone. Thousands of men brought additional stones. Some were rough and tossed aside; some came from the water; some were put in the fire. In her explanation of the parable, the stones represented various Christian lives – the smooth ones were the faithful; the stones from the water represented those who had suffered; the rough ones were those who had fallen away; the ones tossed aside were still close to the tower and could repent; those in the fire were doomed. Around the tower were seven women representing qualities of Faith, Self-restraint, Simplicity, Knowledge, Innocence, Reverence, and Love. Since the tower was a work-in-progress, people had time to embody the qualities and have a place in the tower.

1. The polished stones go into the Tower, 2. Other stones are fitted into the Tower, 3. Some stones pulled down from the Tower are cast away to a distance. 4. Other stones lie around the building unused because they are rough, have cracks, or are the wrong shape or size. These can repent and enter. 5. Some who are very bad are cast at a distance and are placed in an inferior place (outside the light of the City). If these stones repent before Tower is finished, there is a chance for them to be included. 6 Those who are so evil, go further away, dammed to hell (unsaved). Change can happen until the Tower is complete!

"Do you not know that those who run in a race all run, but one receives the prize. Run in such a way that you may obtain it. And everyone who competes for the prize is temperate in all things. Now they do it to obtain a

perishable crown, but we for an imperishable crown. Therefore, I run thus, not with uncertainty. Thus, I fight; not as one who beats the air. But I discipline my body and bring it into subjection lest, when I have preached to others, I myself should become a castaway." (1 Corinthians 9:24-27)

"Coming to Him as to a living stone, rejected indeed by men, but chosen by God and precious, you also, as living stones, are being built up a spiritual house, a holy priesthood, to offer up spiritual sacrifices acceptable to God through Jesus Christ." (1 Peter 2:4-5)

"There is one glory of the sun, and another glory of the moon, and another glory of the stars; for star differs from star in glory. So also, is the resurrection of the dead." (1 Corinthians 15:41)

There is a saying among the Rabbis very like that of the apostle in Yalcut Simeoni, page 2, fol. 10, 'The faces of the righteous shall be, in the world to come, like suns, moons, the heavens, stars, lightnings; and like the lilies and candlesticks of the temple.'

Stones
of
Spiritual
Atmosphere

The river flows from where the veil sits at the edge of the throne. The sapphire throne is a storehouse of treasure, spiritual life, and where creations come forth. Because of who God is, He is always creating by His spirit, unfolding the mysteries from the "stones of fire" that are inside Him (Ezekiel 28:14). His spirit presence flows out of Himself, and living water flows down out of the throne. As shakings and thunders and lightning spark from the throne, precious stones of all spiritual types flow out of God, reflecting His nature, growing and forming in the crystal river that flows down into Eden.

> *"And he showed me a pure river of water of life, as clear as crystal." (Revelation 22)*

Everything that is created has a token, a representation yoked in a precious stone. That being, whatever reflects God's nature and character, which is seen in His sons' or daughters' hearts and achievements and transformations (for where your heart is your treasure shall be). Some stones reflect God's spiritual atmosphere of creation, life, growth, peace, beauty, glory, righteousness, health, and kingdom ownership.

These stones first flowed down from the throne to the Garden in Eden, as Adam and Eve cultivated 'Heaven's atmosphere' in the Garden. As they did this, stones were formed in the river, holding the vibration of Heaven's atmosphere. The stones were a record of transformation and a 'seed of creation' to reflect and manifest God's glory.

Every coloured stone has a different meaning and purpose, and they reflect the rainbow river of God.

A Child's testimony,

"Jesus walked with me to the Rainbow River, and we meet King Solomon there. He gave me a blue gem and told me to throw it into the blue part of the Rainbow River. So, I did. I get lots of different coloured stones from King Solomon. He tells me to put them in the part of the river that matches the stones. 'What do the stones mean?' I asked King Solomon one day. 'Every stone has a meaning behind it,' he said. 'Each one will have a positive influence over the campus. I'll tell you the meaning of the colours each time I give you one. Today's stone is blue, which means it will bring more water and rain to the campus.' The next day, I met King Solomon again. He gave me a green coloured stone. 'Put it in the green part of the river,' he said, 'Green is for growth for the flowers and trees on the campus.'" [68]

So, there are stones that speak about 'us' as we are, 'living stones' being transformed into His image. There are stones that have been 'formed' by God, and stones that represent our prayers to be released into creation to bring life. The meanings of the stones and their colours can change all the time, as this confuses the enemy, who watches these stones 'form' in the earth. It means that when stones are given to us, they reflect our giftings and strengths, and the enemy can't unlock the codes or see what we carry.

Today, as we cultivate Heaven on earth, these stones are being created, released, and 'formed' in the river flowing from the throne. Some are stones representing 'us' (our characters, hearts, tears, spiritual works, rewards, and giftings). Some stones

[68] Angela Curtis, p. 73

represent the adding, transformation, and abiding vibration of Heaven's atmospheres.

As these stones are created, released and flow in the river to the earth and settle behind the veil. Wherever Heaven is established, the spiritual plane behind the veil, behind the material world, will be flooded with spiritual stones. Some will show ownership of areas in the spirit, while others will add spiritual life to that area (like spiritual seeds), like a beacon pulsating presence. Some stones will come through the veil and materialise on earth as reflections of Heaven; as signs and wonders of the age to come, where the new Heaven and New Earth will merge into one creation.

As Adam and Eve cultivated their hearts, stones were formed in the river. Scripture says that our "souls are like a well-watered garden, and like a spring of water, whose waters do not fail." (Isaiah 58:11). As we pray for Heaven to be manifest on earth and transform our characters into the will of God and His nature, our hearts become one in Him. Our lives create and release stones into the spiritual atmosphere. For where your heart is, there your treasure shall be (Matthew 6:21).

Our stones will be many. Some stored in Heaven and others released on earth. We are not to store earthly treasures on earth because this is worldly wealth that robs the heart and focus from seeing the Kingdom (Matthew 6:19), but we are to store up spiritual treasure that records, shapes and vibrates the atmosphere of Heaven to manifest the Kingdom.

Wherever Heaven is cultivated on earth, an over-laying, overshadowing Kingdom will be built behind the veil. In spirit, beautiful rainbow pillars, spirals, towers, and gardens will grow around us, as Eden is manifest in the earth. Each person creates an ecosystem around their lives and where they live.

Lucifer, when he walked with God, stones were his covering; this was because he reflected the heart and nature of God and shone the revelation into creation. This is why he could walk in the midst of the "stones of fire". The stones of fire are not the stones that are manifesting today; they are the eternal stones of God's eternal mysteries of who He is and reflects the revelation of Himself. The stones manifesting today, are a token, a treasure, a reflection of a spark and vibration; a glory of who God's sons and daughters are, and the manifold wisdom of God and His heartbeat, manifesting in His Kingdom.

Seated
in
Heavenly
Places

While I stayed in India, at the Orphanage home that was living under a true open Heaven, I saw in some measure what it means to be 'seated in Heavenly places'. Whether we know it or not, or notice it or not, if we are born again, we are living in two worlds at the same time, constantly. While on earth, our spirit body appears in Heaven without many of us knowing. We can also be doing activities on earth that we are in fact doing in Heaven. I saw this worked out very clearly as I watched the children in their Heavenly visions.

> *"And raised us up together, and made us sit together in the heavenly places in Christ Jesus." (Ephesians 2:6)*

I was in the prayer room one night, praying for the young boys, and as I prayed for many, they would fall down and be in visions on the ground; their spirit bodies were in Heaven translocated. Then suddenly, they got up with their eyes closed, one row kneeling, and another row standing behind, taking turns to fire arrows from their invisible archery bows. The bottom row would fire, then the top all in perfect harmony.

While their physical bodies were on earth, their spirit bodies were in the Heavens doing warfare training.

Dinah Dye says,

> *"Adjacent to his royal complex, King Solomon built a stone-walled, rectangular-shaped forest house for storing armour... (Isaiah. 22:8) It has been suggested that the House of the Forest of Lebanon followed the tripartite layout of the Temple, in that, the Hall of the Pillars correspond to the porch, the forest chamber to*

*the Holy Place (the garden), and the Hall of Judgment
to the Holy of Holies (Eden)."* [69]

As below, so above, the children had gone to the armoury in
the Garden in Heaven.

Another account of this activity:

The young girls were once outside playing in a group with a
ball when suddenly they were caught up in visions in Heaven.
With all their eyes closed, they started hitting a volleyball over a
net, back and forth. This would be impossible in the natural, but
not if they were doing this in Heaven with their eyes open. The
verse, on earth as it is in Heaven, comes to mind.

When we are sleeping, there are times that we can be doing
battle in the Heavens with the Lord. I have friends, who do this,
and at times they wake up the following morning with sore arms
and shoulders from doing battle with swords. Sometimes our
dreams are real battles, in real spiritual places.

*"For we do not wrestle against flesh and blood, but
against principalities, against powers, against the
rulers of the darkness of this age, against spiritual hosts
of wickedness in the heavenly places."* (Ephesians 6:12)

I have also seen spiritual objects appear, such as precious
stones in children's hands, as they receive them in Heaven. When
they come out of their visions, they open their hands, and the
stones are there. At first, these stones didn't manifest in our
realm; they were in other dimensions. Each time they went up,
Jesus kept encouraging them to keep praying, for the stones

---

[69] Dinah Dye, p. 64

would come through the spiritual veil into the natural world in time, and they did...

My friend reports,

> *"From the early days, the children tried to bring back from their visits to Heaven many kinds of Heavenly treasures, including heavenly stones. We saw many looks of bewilderment on the faces of returning children, as the stones that were so real in the spiritual Kingdom were now not present in this natural world. We prompted them to ask Jesus about this. In Heaven, Jesus told a group of visiting children, 'Keep praying, one day they will come through'. It took two years of focused prayer before the breakthrough came.*
>
> *"One night, when we were having our regular Heaven prayer, our daughter walked up to my wife and I with her eyes closed while in a Heavenly trance. She said, 'Mum, this is from Jesus.' She then opened her hand and in it was a beautifully faceted stone, resembling a diamond. She then closed her hand and came over to me and said, 'Dad, this is from Jesus.' She then opened her hand again, and there was a second stone of the same shape and size. When she returned from her heavenly experience, she confirmed that Jesus had personally given her two stones to deliver to my wife and I. She was overwhelmed with joy to learn that the stones had actually come through after many months of trying. Before our very eyes, we witnessed an amazing miracle; the spiritual substance had become a physical substance."*[70]

---

[70] Richard Fellows, *Wilderness like Eden*, p. 23

Healing leaves can also come down from Heaven and be eaten and manifest supernatural healing. Revelation 22:2 speaks about them being in the Heavenly City and says that 'the leaves of the Tree were for the healing of the nations.' Just as precious stones can appear on earth from Heaven through the veil, these healing leaves can float down in the river and can manifest on earth. At this stage, a physical leaf has not appeared. They have been brought down in children's hands yet stayed behind the veil. The children can see them in their hands, but others at this stage have to eat them by faith.

A friend reports,

> "Day by day, my eyes continued to dim and play tricks on me. Colours faded, and I struggled to recognise people at a distance. The television confirmed what I already knew. I could hardly read the subtitles…One evening, when the children were having Heaven prayer, I was caring for the babies and only half participating. Suddenly, Chris walked towards me with her eyes closed and gave me something. 'Eat them,' she said. 'Jesus said there are for you.' 'What are they?' I asked. 'Two red healing leaves.' In faith, I received the unseen leaves, put them to my mouth, chewed and shallowed… Once the children were tucked up away in bed, I returned to our house and turned on the television. To my amazement, the picture looked different, I could see and read everything, and the colours were much stronger, my eyes were prefect." [71]

---

[71] Angela Curtis, p. 109

In the book 'Leaves from the Garden of Eden', a Jewish tale is retold,

> *'In the title of this compendium, an orphaned stable boy named Hayim dies and later appears to his former employer, Shepsel, in a dream. Hayim promises to bring leaves from Eden that can cure any illness. Shepsel awakens to find the fragrant leaves scattered on his bed. He boils them with water and takes the tea to his ailing daughter, who is miraculously healed. Soon she marries and bears a son she names Hayim."* [72]

---

[72] https://umsl.edu/~schwartzh/LeavesJPostrev.html (Accessed 18/4/2021)

The Living Crown of Life

We are told in Scripture that if we are faithful throughout our lives, we will receive the Crown of Life. This doesn't mean we will be excluded if we make a mistake or endure trials, but we are told that there is a 'Crown of Life' for those who keep running the race faithfully.

> *"Be faithful until death, and I will give you the crown of life" (Revelation 2:10)*

On reading this verse, we must go another layer deeper. Not only do we receive a crown, but it is also a crown about our life, and it's alive and moving. Testimony has revealed that this Crown grows throughout our lives, and Jesus adds to it as we accomplish victories and assignments. This Crown is a crown of our life's history on earth, and it is living, moving and interacting with our heartbeat. In the Crown are tokens, symbols, precious stones, and Heavenly objects that tell the testimony of our lives. In Heaven, our crown will appear on our heads as we come to the throne. In worship, many lay their crowns down before the Throne, and those crowns will dance/speak forth, move in front of Him, and tell the stories of our lives, of what we have overcome by God's Grace for His Glory.

> *"They lay their crowns before the throne." (Revelation 4:9-10)*

The crown the believer obtains, is the victor's crown (Greek - *stephanos*). Historically, a perishable wreath was given for victory in the games, achievements in war, and places of honour. In contrast, the crown the believer obtains from God is eternal and comes from faithfulness, and as one can lose other crowns, this one is the story of our life that we will place before the King each time we come to the Throne, manifesting in a living 'art form' His glory in us. So, we must walk carefully...

There are other crowns that can be merited: the crown of glory for special recognition for Shepherding the flock (1 Peter 5:1-4), and the crown of righteousness for upright behaviour, a righteous life lived (2 Timothy 4:6-8).

Jewish tradition speaks of a place in Heaven called the 'Treasury of Merits', where people are being rewarded for their hardships by the gems being placed into their crowns. Take note of the phrase, 'crowns of life'.

> "So, too, are there treasuries of comfort, where ministering angels sit and weave garments of salvation, making crowns of life and fixing precious stones and pearls to them."[73]

A Heaven encounter reveals more,

> "Crowns were hanging half-finished on hocks and along the shelves. Crates of precious gems and different metals waited for Him to turn them into something precious. 'Would you like to help me?' Jesus asked. 'Yes,' I said...He smiled, and before I could even pick up wire and get started, it appeared before me already bent into a circle, exactly what I had imagined, but without the stones. 'It isn't finished yet,' He said. It was then I realised we were working on my crown. 'With each new accomplishment, a new embellishment will be added to your crown,' He said.... All these crowns are for people still on earth. They are created over time as they experience different seasons and special moments

[73] Howard Schwartz, p. 189

in their lives. Their crowns aren't completed until their time on earth has passed... Each time I visit His workshop, the crown has been added to... it is so beautiful, a moving living crown." [74]

The Crown of Life is not just a sign of a righteous life; it is your life manifesting above your head with the authority and experiences and glory you have become in Him. Your life story is the glory you will bring Him.

Our living crown will be an eternal sign of our journey of life on earth and how we laid our lives down for our God. The children's visions through this book reveal the beauty of God's love towards us; that He is always walking with us, comforting us, even when most of us don't see Him face to face. The children's visions and encounters call us to walk lives worthy of our King Jesus. It matters how we live, as we are called to reflect Him and His likeness on earth. Our love and sacrifices will never be unnoticed but greatly rewarded. Let us set our minds on things above and rise to the high calling of God. Let Heaven through the eyes of these children bring hope, love, faith and grace to go deeper into the mysteries of the eternal Kingdom, God's heartbeat.

---

[74] Angela Curtis, p.87

⌘

Has this book stirred you? Would you like to commit your life to God and follow Jesus as your Saviour?

I would suggest you read the following scriptures:

John 14:6 – *"Jesus said to him, 'I am the way, the truth and the life; no man comes to the Father, except through me."*

Romans 3:23 – *"For all have sinned, and come short of the glory of God."*

John 3:16 – *"For God so loved the world that He gave his only begotten Son, that whosoever believes in Him, will not die, but have eternal life."*

1 Corinthians 15:3,4 – *"Christ died for our sins; He was buried and rose again on the third day according to the Scriptures."*

Ephesians 2:8 – *"For by grace you are saved through faith; and that not of yourselves; it is the gift of God."*

John 1:12,13 – *"As many as received Him, to them He gave the power to become the sons of God, even to them that believe on His name: which were born not of blood, nor the will of the flesh, nor the will of man, but of God."*

Now you will understand that none of us can enter Heaven on our own merits, but only through believing that Jesus Christ has already paid the penalty for your wrongdoings by dying on the cross for you. It's as simple as talking to God, but if you're not sure how, read Psalm 51 aloud, as it is a prayer David prayed to God when he'd sinned.

Now, get your own copy of the Bible (King James Version, or New American Standard versions are pretty accurate translations, but NIV or Passion Translation could be easier to read). And find a Bible-believing fellowship in your community who can help you grow.

Bibliography

Alec, W. (2005) *The Fall of Lucifer*, Warboys Publishing Ltd. (Although this is a fictional novel, it is based on her personal revelations and visions, of which more can be read in her book, Visions of Heaven, listed below.)

Alec, W. (2013) *Visions of Heaven*, Warboys Publishing Ltd.

Clayton, I. (2016) *Realms of the Kindom, Volume One*, Sons of Thunder Publications.

Curtis, A. (2019) *Talk With Me in Paradise*, Kin & Kingdom Books.

Cauley, M (2012) *The Outer Darkness*, Misthological Press.

Dillow, J. (2018) *Final Destiny, The Future Reign of the Servant Kings*, Grace Theology Press.

Dye, D. (2015) *The Temple in the Garden*; Priests and Kings, Foundations of Torah.

Fellows, R. (2019) *Wilderness Like Eden*, WordWyze Publishing.

Fellows, R. (2019) *Granny Rainbow Shekinah*, WordWyze Publishing.

Missler, C. (2007) *The Kingdom, Power & Glory*, The Kings High Way Ministries, Inc.

Parson, M. (2018) *My Journey Beyond Beyond*, Choir Press.

Raphaels, S. (2019) *Jewish Views of the Afterlife*, Rowan & Littlefield.

Rokser, D. (2015) *Should Christians Fear Outer Darkness*, Grace Gospel Press.

Schwartz, H. (2004) *Tree of Souls, the Mythology of Judaism*, Oxford University Press.

Scott, E. (2008) *40 Days in Heaven*, First Fruits Offering Printing.

Shmuel, *The Ocean of Tears*, Tikkun, accessed 22 Apr 2021, http://loveisthemotive.blogspot.com/2014/10/the-ocean-of-tears.html

Woodworth-Etter, M. (1980) *A Diary of Signs and Wonders,* Harrison House Inc

Other books by Richard Fellows, available online or direct from the author – richfellows@hotmail.com

Wilderness Like Eden (2019) ISBN 978-0-648-58830-6

The supernatural appearing of gemstones from Heaven, around the world, is on the increase as faithful Christians worship God and cry out for the joining of Heaven and earth. What is the phenomenon? How is it related to the God of the Bible?

In Wilderness Like Eden, these questions are addressed in the light of God's Heavenly Kingdom intimately clothing Eden, the Bride and the Sons of God – their functions and callings in the earth.

Granny Rainbow Shekinah (2019) ISBN 978-0-648-58832-0

Throughout history, God has revealed Himself in His creation. In The Garden of Eden, he visited earth in Theophanies in the Old Testament, in the incarnation of Jesus, and also in disguise, after His resurrection and ascension into Heaven. But what of the Holy Spirit, what is His image and likeness? What is the Holy Spirit's "form" and essence as the Spirit of Glory?

In Granny Rainbow Shekinah, these questions and more are addressed. Come on a journey as we go behind the veil!